KATHY SMITH CARTER

TOLERATED
NOT WANTED

FINDING **GOD** IN THE AFTERMATH
OF CHILDHOOD TRAUMA

Tolerated Not Wanted: Finding God in the Aftermath of Childhood Trauma

© 2020 by Kathy Smith Carter

For more information, email toleratednotwanted@gmail.com

ISBN: 978-1-7349227-0-7 (paperback)

ISBN: 978-1-7349227-1-4 (ebook)

Dedication

To the adults who are struggling with depression
and anxiety as a result of being different: There is hope.

To the teenager who struggles with teasing or bullying and feels
so alone: You are not alone.

To the person who feels hopeless: There is always a way out.

To the children of God who feel unworthy and unforgivable:
God's grace covers you.

And to ichthyosis patients and parents, there is a way
to rise above.

Contents

Introduction

I want to begin by saying that this is not my story. Well, it is my story, but it is really a story of how God helped me go from broken to whole and from hurting to healed. If you have ever felt different or socially ostracized, this book was written for you. If you have ever found yourself feeling hopeless, this book was written for you. And if you consider yourself a believer but find yourself very far from God, this book was written for you.

But first, let me introduce myself. I am currently forty-nine years old and an elementary school counselor. I have been married for twenty years to my best friend and biggest supporter, Greg, who is in a wheelchair due to polio. I am a mom to three Labrador retrievers, which I have trained as therapy dogs and take to school with me weekly. They serve as therapy to both the children and the staff at my school. I am the youngest of three girls and have a close relationship with both of my sisters. My father is deceased, but my mother is still a consistent, positive part of my life.

In this book, I will not only tell you about a skin disease I was born with but also how it affected my body, heart, and mind. I do not want sympathy, and in fact, I won't accept it. I was born this way, and this is all I know. As a result of my skin disease, I developed problems making friends and interacting in social situations. I was the kid no one wanted to touch or sit beside. They said things like I was gross, I needed to take a bath, and I smelled bad. My beliefs about myself were undermined by ridicule and isolation.

In addition to my skin disease, I made some regretful decisions and developed some bad habits. Over time, these issues morphed into some huge problems with my beliefs about myself and about God. Though I was raised in the church, I found myself far from the God I learned about there and in Sunday school and youth group. As recently as a couple of years ago, I was depressed, anxious, and hopeless. I had been told my whole life that God would never leave me or forsake me (Deuteronomy 41:10), but I couldn't find him. Somewhere in the back of my mind, I knew God loved me, but I didn't feel it. Neither did I love myself—I believed I was unforgivable, defective, and unlovable. Although I was moral—looking good on the outside—and talked like a believer, I didn't give God the time of day.

When God asked me to write my story, I argued with him. I told him that I would tell my testimony. The answer I got was loud and clear: Nope. Write your story so I can use it to my glory. You see, I have been trying for years to handle life by myself. I had a great deal of pain in my head and my heart, pain that I pushed away and locked up tight. I didn't talk about it or even acknowledge it was there because it hurt too much. I found myself having a great deal of anxiety along with thoughts of self-harm and hopelessness. I spent years trying to handle the pain related to my skin disease by myself. But doing it my way was going to kill me.

I came to a point in my life where something had to change, because if it didn't, I would begin losing things that mattered to me the most. So I began to make some changes. Some were small, and some were big, but they were all difficult and scary. Through a series of winks from God and some much-needed divine strength, I began to fight my way back. With determination laced with fear, I embarked on a path of changing my thinking and my beliefs about myself.

I am not going to lie and tell you it was quick or easy. Nor am I going to tell you that my battles are over. I still have bad days, and I get discouraged and afraid occasionally. But I have some strategies that have helped me that I want to share with you. None of them involve rocket science, and in fact, most of them are quite basic. But I am convinced that sometimes we all need to get back to the basics.

My story is a story filled with pain, spiritual battles, and difficult challenges. It is an account of a victory—a battle that Jesus wins and pain that God heals—that I want to share with you. It is my testimony of overcoming obstacles and fighting the enemy to live the life God wants for me. Some of what I reveal in this book is painful and embarrassing, but I share it with you because I know that I am not the only one in the world who has felt helpless and hopeless. I share it because others have also been teased, shunned, or ostracized due to a disability or physical trait. My hope is that you will be able to relate to my stories and my pain. My prayer is that the things I have learned can help you win your own battle.

I hope you can bear with me as I describe my disease and resulting challenges. It is quite unique (if I do say so myself). Wait till I tell you about my superpower! Unless you know the facts about my disease, you won't be able to understand the battle I fought. Rest assured, this story is true and sometimes difficult to read. But the ending will offer you a sense of hope and encourage you to take steps toward getting yourself back on track. You are never alone in whatever battle you are fighting, and there is always, always, always hope!

So, buckle up. Let's get going!

What Is Wrong with Your Skin?

For you created my inmost being;
you knit me together in my mother's womb.
I praise you because I am fearfully and wonderfully made;
your works are wonderful,
I know that full well.
My frame was not hidden from you
when I was made in the secret place,
when I was woven together in the depths of the earth.
Your eyes saw my unformed body;
all the days ordained for me were written in your book
before one of them came to be.

– Psalm 139:13–16 (NIV)

The first thing that most people remark about my skin is "Wow! You have been out in the sun. You've got a bad sunburn." I usually smile and reply that it is a skin condition I was born with. I tell them my skin is very dry and thin, and I explain that I get hurt easily but heal very quickly. I often say, "If I hit the edge of the table with the back of my hand, it would rip the skin off my hand." They usually respond with an embarrassed apology of some sort. I am not offended though, as it is a question I am quite used to answering.

But I am getting ahead of myself. Let me first explain the basics of the disease, then I will get into my own experiences.

Two in a Million

My skin disease is called *ichthyosis* (ik-thee-O-sis). That term actually describes over twenty different skin diseases, all of which involve dry, scaly, rough skin. The word *ichthyosis* comes from the Latin word *ichthy* which means "fish." So it makes sense that it can look like fish or alligator scales. Studies estimate that about sixteen thousand people are born with ichthyosis every year. Out of those, about three hundred cases of the disease are considered moderate to severe. It is sometimes present from birth but can develop later in life as well.

I was born with epidermolytic ichthyosis, a type of ichthyosis that occurs in about two out of a million people. As a small child, my friends enjoyed getting me to say the term aloud that doctors in the '70s had taught me: "epidermolytic ichthyosis hyperkeratosis." I would say it in short sound bites, and they would try to repeat it. "Epi . . . dermo . . . lytic . . . ichthy . . . osis . . . hyper . . . kera . . . tosis." We would laugh and giggle as they failed to repeat it correctly every time. They were amazed that someone so young could say such a complicated string of words. Doctors have since added the term *bullous variety* to my diagnosis as well. If you break the terms down, here is what they mean:

- *Epidermolytic* refers to the reddish blistering.
- *Ichthyosis* refers to the fish-like scales.
- *Hyperkeratosis* refers to the thickening of the skin.
- *Bullous* refers to blistering.

My skin is dry, red, easily blistered, prone to infection, thick, smelly, and itchy. I'm not sure if you picked up on that word *smelly*, but as a child, my skin did not smell good. With all the thick scales, it is common for bacteria to grow around and under the scales, causing a distinct odor. As you can imagine, this caused many problems for me growing up. You will hear more about that later.

Dry and Scaly

Ichthyosis skin does not have the barrier it needs to hold in moisture, so patients experience lots of dry, scaly skin. The skin builds up to very thick, almost warty-looking scales. These scales are worse on any joint areas, such as the hands, feet, knees, hips, waist, neck, and elbows. The scales can be very painful and require lots of added moisture to keep them pliable. All skin sheds constantly, but normal skin sheds in tiny microscopic pieces, while ichthyosis skin sheds in visible pieces of considerable size.

Blisters

Another characteristic of epidermolytic ichthyosis is frequent blistering. This can occur with repetitive motion or as a result of contact. Blisters are often caused by walking, standing, sitting, and contact with clothing, shoes, and any hard surfaces. Even contact with soft surfaces can cause blisters. Blisters often lead to an increased risk of infection, which can be a constant battle.

Overheating

Ichthyosis affects the body's ability to regulate body temperature. Think of sweat or perspiration as the skin's natural way of lowering the body temperature by releasing hot moisture. Since people with ichthyosis do not sweat properly, all the heat gets trapped inside the body. Once we begin to get hot, we have difficulty cooling off. We become almost like a walking sauna. Since getting too hot can cause a heat stroke, ichthyosis patients must be very careful not to overheat. If we do get hot, we must have access to immediate and quick-acting methods of cooling.

Cause and treatment

Doctors tell me that my ichthyosis is a result of a genetic mutation and that there is no cure. It can be genetically inherited, but since there is no history of it in my family, a mutation makes the most sense. Since it is genetic, it can be passed to my future children through my genes. This is *part* of the reason I have chosen not to have children. (I'll talk about that in chapter 3). And just for the record, you can't "catch" it from someone.

Because there is no cure for ichthyosis, the goal is to manage the symptoms. Treatment options include the application of a moisture barrier and topical ointments that decrease the thickness of the skin. Exfoliating and oral medications are often routine as well. Although I have never personally met anyone else with ichthyosis, I do have contact with some through social media. From what I can tell, we all have different methods for managing our symptoms. I will describe my own treatment efforts in the next section.

My Experience with Ichthyosis

Now that I have given you a general overview, I want to take some time to tell you about my ichthyosis. I have never met someone that has this disease, so I am not sure how others experience it. From what I have read on social media, every case is different.

Infancy

My mom first noticed something was wrong when her water broke and hundreds of pieces of skin were in it. I was born with a hard shell covering my body. My mom said it felt like tapping a turtle shell. Within a few days, this shell peeled off and left my skin completely raw. My skin was then bright red, raw, and oozing this clear plasma-like substance. (Sorry for the gross stuff—it won't be the last time.) One doctor told my parents I would die if they took me home. Another said that it was fine to take me home. But after two weeks in the NICU, I came home with my parents and my two older sisters.

When I did come home from the hospital, my parents had no idea what to do. Neither did the doctors. It was such a rare disease that very little was known about it. My parents carried me on a pillow and laid me on a beanbag or a bouncy seat made of cloth. They were not able to hold me because any physical touch hurt my sores or ripped my skin. I wasn't held while I ate or slept. A great deal of trial and error was involved. There were problems with mattresses, clothes, and even diapers.

Bath Time

My mom has asked me if I remember bath time, and thankfully, I do not. My skin was easily ripped, so typical childhood activities led to lots of deep, raw sores. I could bump a wall or a table with any part of my body and rip large areas of skin. When the water touched my open sores, I screamed in pain. My sisters would go outside and play during my bath time because they could not stand to hear me scream. They confess now that they thought my mom was torturing me. I am grateful that God did not let me remember.

However, I do remember when I was elementary school age and had to get in the bathtub with my socks or pants on because my sores were stuck to the fabric. Until my sores could build the first protective layer, they would ooze. This ooze would soil my socks or clothes. If the sore was in a place that was in constant contact with my clothing, it would stick to the fabric. Several times a month my skin would heal as part of whatever fabric I was wearing. When I got in the tub, I would take a deep breath and brace myself for the pain of the water hitting my sores. Removing the dry fabric would mean ripping off the skin completely, so by wetting the fabric, I stood a better chance of causing less damage. If I took it slow, I could separate skin and cloth, ripping off only about half the healing skin instead of all of it.

Bath time is always followed by immediate head-to-toe moisturizing. My daily routine continues to be showering and covering my body in oil once or twice a day.

Clothes

Finding clothes that do not hurt my skin has been a big ordeal since day one. My clothes must be loose and soft. I am the person you see in the stores walking around touching everything. The softer the clothing, the better I like it. Cotton or fleece work best. My clothes are a size or two too big because anything tight will rip my skin. My pants must all have an elastic waist, but the elastic cannot be tight. Pants run the risk of ripping my skin around the waist or the seams. Shirts with cuffs on the wrists or around the neck can cause a problem. Socks and other undergarments are major difficulties as well. Although I long to keep up with the latest fashions, I am forced to do what works for me.

The trickiest issue related to clothing has always been shoes. Tennis shoes, boots, dress shoes, heels, and even flip-flops are all out of the question. I remember wearing footies and moccasins to church as a child and transitioning to sandals as I grew up. I have always wanted to fit in and wear what others were wearing. To this day, I am jealous of you ladies that can wear cool, colorful, sneakers or calf-high boots and leggings — I call it "shoe envy."

I would like to give a shout out to the people that make Crocs because they are the only shoes I can wear right now. Since Crocs are designed to slip on and off, I can get them loose enough not to even touch my foot when I am standing. Let me go ahead and make this official: I would like to take credit for making Crocs cool again! I have Crocs that match almost any outfit and own about thirty pairs. I wear my light-up Christmas Crocs in December, my Tie-Dye Crocs during summer, and my Mickey Mouse Crocs at work. They make me happy. And yes, I buy goofy Jibbitz to decorate many of my Crocs. I have butterflies, flowers, Disney characters, and Alabama Crimson Tide Jibbitz. I get very excited about decorating my Crocs and get quite a bit of joy from doing so. I could talk about my Croc collection all day, so don't get me started.

My Superpower

One thing I find ironic is that although my skin can be thick and scaly it also heals very quickly. My skin is easily torn or blistered but heals four or five times faster than normal skin. I call this rapid healing my superpower. If there was one cool thing about my disease, this would be it. I can go to bed with blisters and after nine to ten hours of sleep they will be gone. Sleep is critical though. If I don't get enough sleep and don't have a super-soft surface to sleep on, my superpower is diminished. Let me give you a couple of stories to illustrate.

One Christmas Eve when I was five, I fell backward over a trash bag in our kitchen, slicing the back of my leg on some broken glass that was in the bag. I ended up in the emergency room of our local children's hospital, sitting on a towel and waiting for the doctor. There was another child there on that same night who was having some type of severe skin reaction. My dad told me that the doctor came into my room and began asking him and my mom all about my skin.

"What is it called? How long has she had it? What are the symptoms? What medications have you tried?"—question after question about my skin. My parents thought it was rather odd that he was asking so many questions, but they answered them patiently. Finally, the doctor looked at my parents and said, "It's Christmas Eve. What in the hell do you want me to do about it?" Apparently, he saw my skin and assumed I was the skin reaction patient, an honest mistake. I imagine he felt rather foolish when they told him I was there to have my leg sewn up. We still laugh about that incident today. I have a Donald Duck doll that has the following words written on it: "Kathy got this and 7 stitches on Dec. 24, 1976."

The craziest part of the story is that my dermatologist had to come to my house the following day (Christmas) and take the stitches out. It seems that in 1976 they did not have dissolvable stitches. In less than eighteen hours, my skin was healing *over* the stitches.

On another occasion, I woke my dog suddenly, and he jumped up, accidentally cutting my eye with his tooth. When we arrived at the hospital, they told us that I needed stitches but the doctor was busy so it would be a while. By the time the doctor did get to me, I didn't need stitches anymore. It had healed.

Struggling to Stay Cool

As I mentioned earlier, heat is a huge problem for me. My parents installed a pool when I was small, and that allowed me to spend time outside in the summer. For a few years we had a giant heated dome over our pool, which allowed me to swim in winter. Not only does the pool act as a coolant in hot weather but it also helps replenish the moisture in my skin. However, my skin dries out quickly when I get out of the water. Whether it be the shower or the pool, I have to hurry and cover myself in some type of cold cream or oil to hold in the moisture, otherwise my skin gets tight and painful.

As a child, I constantly feared overheating, which caused me a great deal of anxiety. I remember thinking on school field trips, *What if it is too hot, and no one will listen to me? What if I overheat while playing at school, and no one understands the seriousness of the situation? What if I find myself in a situation where I don't have a way to cool off?* It was always on my mind back then and has remained an ever-present issue as my ability to cope with heat has decreased with age.

I still have a pool today, and it allows me to go outside in the summer. Since my husband is in a wheelchair, most of the outside chores fall on my shoulders. If the temperature is too warm, I will have to take frequent dips in the pool to keep cool.

I have tried many things over the years to stay cool that haven't quite worked out. I experimented with a cooling vest that holds something like ice packs against my skin, but for it to work, it had to be so snug it ripped my skin. Cooling towels and hats aren't quite enough either. I have, however, found some adaptations that help. For example, long sleeve swim shirts are perfect for me—I wet a shirt, put it on, and mow the grass. I also carry a squirt bottle with me to wet my shirt and hair when I get hot. (If someone out there can please design a way to attach a squirt bottle to a lawn mower, I would appreciate it.)

Not too long ago, I went to Disney World with my family. We were faced with temperatures in the upper eighties. I pretty much stayed wet the entire trip. When I dried, I would go into the bathroom and rewet my swim shirt. There were a few times when my family had to pour ice water, which we kept with us in a cooler, on my head or down my back.

Hot cars are exceptionally dangerous for me, and running errands in the summer can be a problem. I get hot walking to the car, then I have to get into an even hotter car. Most of the time, the car doesn't have time to cool off before I get to my next destination, so my body heats up by the minute. I do have a remote start on my car so I can get the A/C going before I even go outside, but when the temperature rises to the nineties, my husband must be my chauffeur. He drives and keeps the car cool, dropping me off and waiting for me at the door.

There have been times when I have had to put ice packs under my arms, on the back of my neck, or on my wrists. I have done this on airplanes, in restaurants, and of course, outside. If I am home, the pool is my best friend. If you have a pool, you know that sometimes even the pool gets too warm. In these cases, I end up with my head under a garden hose.

In sum, I can get warm, but if I do not have immediate access to a rapid cooling method, problems will occur. And once I overheat, I will find myself exhausted and wiped out for the rest of the day. I have learned to adapt, think ahead, and plan for potential emergencies. I manage just fine, but needless to say, winter is my favorite time of the year.

Blisters and Sores

Blisters are an everyday occurrence in my world. Sometimes they are caused by infection, but most of the time they are caused by friction. Remember that I mentioned my skin can be thick and scaly? At the same time, it is very brittle and easily ripped. This means that even a slight bump of a table or a counter will rip my skin. I love to work outside in my yard, but I will inevitably have many self-inflicted sores on different parts of my body. The more sores I have, the more likely I will get an infection. There are times when numerous scrapes on my arms and legs led to big problems.

To help prevent sores, I prefer to wear long pants and long sleeves. Of course, that isn't possible all year round, but I try such things as keeping my house cool so that I can wear clothing to protect me. I cut my fingernails almost daily so as not to scratch myself. My dogs are trained to keep their paws on the ground so that they don't hurt me. I often have people ask me if my dogs can shake hands. I explain to them that "shake" is a trick I will not teach my dogs because this teaches them to use their paws to communicate with humans. The last thing I need is a dog that scratches me and creates more sores. While I am a dog lover to the core, being around dogs who jump on me or paw at me can ruin my day.

With movement or friction, the outer layers of my skin will separate from my body and fill with liquid. If popped, there is raw skin underneath. Is it painful? Absolutely. Pain is a daily part of my life. My skin can get so sore as it nears the point of blistering that it hurts to move. It is a pain that is difficult for others to understand so I try to hide it as often as I can. Even after twenty years of marriage, my husband will hear me wince as I get up off the couch at night. Not too long ago, he asked, "Does it really hurt that bad?" Even after all this time, he still struggles to understand. I feel my best in the mornings and the worst in the evenings.

The pain is not something I talk about often because it is there all the time. If I mentioned it every time I hurt, it would be all I talked about. By the end of most days, just adjusting my body on the couch or turning over in bed can be excruciating. Sometimes it is an article of clothing that causes blisters. Other times they just happen without any reason. Truthfully, I could be completely naked all day and still get blisters.

As I mentioned earlier, my skin gets thicker around my joints and any repetitive motion can cause blisters. Changing gears in a manual transmission car or riding a bicycle rips the skin on the back of my knees. If I sit too long, I get blisters on my back or the back of my legs. If I stand or walk too long, I get blisters on my feet or my knees. A perfect day for me is a balance of sitting, standing, and lying on a soft surface. Granted, those perfect days don't happen very often.

Cushions and memory foam mattresses are my friends. Hospital beds are my nemesis. Any time I have to be admitted to the hospital, I can expect to be in more than my usual pain. I have tried laying an air mattress over the hospital mattress with lots of blankets, but the longer I am there, the more pain I am in.

Then there are the times when I have blisters pop out all over my back or my arms for no apparent reason. If I have too many sores and too much infection for my body to fight, blisters will appear out of nowhere. My husband and I have watched as hundreds of blisters have appeared before our very eyes. I was recently in the hospital for ulcers, and the tops of my feet blistered like bubble wrap. I'm still not sure what that was about!

Car rides often cause problems for me because of the friction between my skin and the seat. I can help reduce some of this friction with blankets and pillows, but ultimately, there is only so much I can do. When going on a several-hour car ride, I can plan on being sore and possibly blistered by the time I arrive. On our trips to the beach, I often drive the last hour so that I can use the steering wheel to hold myself away from the seat. Even laying my arm on an armrest will cause blisters. Training seminars, conferences, and airplane rides are a challenge, as is anything fun.

My mother and I often have arguments over my desire to do things that I know are going to hurt. Sometimes it is out of necessity, such as when I have to pull weeds or mow the grass. Mom will often say, "Why do you do that to yourself?" to which I respond, "Who else is going to do it?" Because my husband is in a wheelchair, there are many things he cannot do, despite the fact that we have made our property as handicapped-friendly as possible. So, much to my mother's chagrin, I often hurt myself doing work that must be done. And until educators earn significantly higher wages, I will continue to be doing the work myself.

But other times, I do things I know will hurt because I want and need to have fun. I roller skate knowing I will pay for it later. I snow ski and jet ski, even though there will be repercussions. My choice is either to stay inside and avoid doing things that are going to hurt or have some fun and take ibuprofen later. My poor mother aches for me during these times, but I want to live! I want to have some fun! (I would like to note here that my philosophy of living life on ibuprofen has led to a few stomach ulcers, so I have had to switch to acetaminophen. Lesson learned.)

Living in a Snow Globe

Have you watched the TV commercials for dandruff shampoo where people complain about embarrassing flakes? Close your eyes and imagine having dandruff over your entire body. Now imagine that the flakes are much, much bigger, hundreds of them coming off all the time.

Let that sink in for a moment.

Flakes are coming out of your hair, your ears, your face, your back, your legs, your hands—everywhere. In my family, we call those flakes *snow*. Hey, why not use a little humor to cope, right?

Snow is a part of my daily existence. It is everywhere I go. I peel all the time. My skin falls off—constantly. I tell people that I live in a snow globe. Every time I walk or move or stand or sit, it snows. Every time I take off a sock or a shirt, there is a blizzard on the floor. When I was younger, my sisters would come up to me, shake my clothes, and sing "Let it Snow! Let it Snow! Let it Snow!" I can wave my arm while I'm teaching, and snow will fall out on the floor. The other day I went bowling, and a decent-sized dusting of snow was on the ground where I had spent an hour standing.

I buy all my clothes in light colors, especially my shirts, in an attempt to hide the flakes. If people with dandruff struggle with flakes on a black shirt, imagine my experience with dandruff on steroids! It sounds odd, but I long to wear black or navy or red tops. Yet if I did, I would spend the entire day brushing off snow every few minutes.

Snow falls constantly out of my hair, out of my sleeves, and out of my pant legs! I was horrified when my husband and I bought a house that had just been carpeted with wall-to-wall dark green carpet. *Ugh!* Thankfully, we have since transitioned to a more neutral-tone carpet. However, vacuuming and sweeping are still a frequent occurrence at my house. I am self-conscious when I go to someone's house and they have dark-colored carpet or a black couch. No matter how hard I try, snow happens.

One time I went to a lunch meeting with the principals in my school district, and the tablecloths were black. I texted a friend and told her my situation, and she responded, "Don't move! Be very, very still!" On another occasion, I went to a conference where every chair and table and tablecloth was—you guessed it—black. I guess it is a good thing I am not prone to criminal activity, because I leave my DNA everywhere.

It is an instinct for me to turn around and wipe off the seat when I stand up because I know I have left evidence that I was there. And you should see my car—I have to vacuum it out every other day. People will often say, "Don't worry about it. It's no big deal." But to me, it is a huge deal. Even in my mother's house, I get the broom and sweep up a snowdrift. I mean, no one else I know leaves a snowstorm everywhere they go.

Are there any compulsive peelers out there? I know people who love to peel sunburns. You can't help yourself. It feels good when it is being pulled off, and it's kind of fun. I'm not alone in that, right? Imagine that, somewhere on your body, large parts of your skin are peeling all the time. I admit that I do peel my skin often, but I try not to do it in public. It can be hard to resist. Occasionally I've been able to peel pieces of skin as long as six inches. Cool, but a little gross.

At times, this peeling causes lots of pain. A few times a year my skin will peel from head to toe. It gets very tight and painful, then it begins to crack all over and come up along the edges of the scales. I imagine a snake might feel like this when its skin molts. I often feel very overwhelmed by the sensation of tight, dry, itchy skin during these times. It is hard not to be cranky because of the pain. The most annoying part of this process is when the palms of my hands peel. It usually starts in a couple of places and proceeds across my entire palm and between my fingers. Talk about a weird sensation!

Other Quirks

For the fun of it, I want to share with you a few other oddities about being me. Some of them I consider to be blessings. Others I see as tolerable annoyances. For instance, I cannot shave my legs or any other part of my body. Can you imagine what running a razor up my calf would do to my leg? I tried it once with an electric razor, and it took hours. Not only that, but the process of the hair growing back was itchy—and I don't need any more itching. If you are around me in the summertime, you likely won't even notice hair on my legs. Since I have only tried to shave once in my life, the hair on my legs is so soft and light-colored that you can't see it. Think of the time I save *not* having to shave my legs.

Makeup is another thing I don't have to spend my time on. Because my skin overturns so quickly, any blush or eyeshadow I put on is gone in a couple of hours. "Concealer" is a joke for me because I would need enough to cover my entire body, and eyeliner doesn't stay put. The last time I wore makeup was on my wedding day.

I can paint my nails, but it, too, is a waste of time. Within less than a day, it is peeling off. I have even tried the new stick-on fingernails with all the latest technologies. Once I spent hours with my sisters getting cute Mickey Mouse nails before a trip to Disney World. They peeled off before I even got into the park the next day. Besides, I have to keep my nails extremely short so that I have less of an opportunity to scratch myself in my sleep.

I remind my husband how much money he saves because I cannot wear jewelry. Rings are either too loose to stay on my finger or so snug that they rip my skin. Necklaces bother the skin on my neck. I tried getting my ears pierced as a teenager, but this was not successful. If I took the earrings out for more than a couple of hours, the holes grew together. If I left them in all the time, they got infected. I have recently tried earrings again and have been able to find a balance that works. Nothing makes me happier than to wear my dog or Mickey Mouse earrings!

Everyone has told me I should never attempt to get a tattoo because of the potential for infection. But one day I got so desperate to do something others can do, I went to the tattoo parlor. I selected a small Mickey Mouse tattoo for my chest. And let me tell you, it hurt! It felt like someone was ripping my skin at a slow, excruciating pace. When the gentleman said that he didn't think it was working, I came flying up out of the chair. It was not worth it. After all that pain, it looks like someone drew on my body with a pen that didn't work very well. My mom says it serves me right.

Treatments

My God will meet all your needs according to the riches of his glory in Christ Jesus.

– Philippians 4:19

When I was born, doctors were not sure what I had, much less knew how to treat it. When I was around four years of age, my parents took me to Emory University and National Institute of Health (NIH) in Maryland. Neither of these hospitals were willing to make any recommendations. I have a brief memory of sitting alone in a room on a metal table at NIH. Several doctors in white coats came in and began holding out my hands, turning my arms, looking at my back. I am not sure where my parents were, but I remember feeling scared. The doctors didn't speak to me or interact with me in any way. They just looked at my skin as if I were a specimen and then left.

There were lots of doctor's visits, antibiotics, and experimental treatments. Infections occurred often, and I got pretty good at knowing when I needed to seek help from my doctor. My doctors became very familiar with me and listened to what I told them about my body. Even now, my dermatologist will take my phone calls when I am out of town or see me on a moment's notice. He knows that I do not ask for help unless it is an emergency.

My mom tells a story of a time when I was a baby and woke up one morning with infected blisters all over my back. She scooped me up and took me straight to my pediatrician's office. She was the first one in the door that morning, but the doctor had not yet arrived. The receptionist explained to my mom that the doctor did not have any openings and that I would not be able to see him. Mom went around to the back of the building and waited until he pulled up in his car. He got out of his car, took us straight in the back door, and we never saw that receptionist there again.

Trial and Error

Doctors told us that I might outgrow my disease at puberty or it might be a lifelong thing. But truthfully, they were just guessing. To this day, people with ichthyosis know more about their disease than their doctors do. There are so many different types of the disease, and no two cases seem to be completely alike. Fortunately, my doctors listened. They wondered if it was a vitamin E deficiency and told me to eat a lot of eggs. I can remember eating three scrambled eggs for breakfast for several of my elementary years. You would think that I hate them now, but they are still one of my favorites. Then doctors conjectured I had a vitamin D deficiency, so they had me stand in a UV lightbox (a '70s version of a tanning bed). All that did was make me hot and scared. I had to stand naked in a room the size of a phone booth with hot lights on three sides, while my mom talked to me through the door.

There is no known cure for ichthyosis, but my doctor left no stone unturned. Every time I left my doctor's office, I was given a bag of different creams and ointments to try. None of them worked though. My mom had several people tell her that if she had more faith I would be cured.

One lady even followed her into the bathroom to tell her that my disease was a result of her sin. Seriously? I have grown weary of people who suggest to me that whatever brand of supplements they are selling is the answer to my problems. I know that they mean well, but I believe if the answer was that simple, my doctor would have found it by now.

My skin itches constantly, and I am unable to control my scratching when I sleep. My parents would make me wear soft gloves at night so I couldn't scratch myself. That didn't work because they would tape them on and I just took them off. To try and hold in the moisture, my parents even coated me with oil then wrapped me in plastic wrap at night. That didn't work either—I took that off too. I began taking an anti-itching medication to help me control my actions when I sleep. This is still a critical part of my nightly routine. Without it, I am likely to make hand size sores on myself when I sleep.

The scented lotions of today are a waste of time when it comes to keeping my skin moisturized. All they really do is give me a good scent for about thirty minutes, while the moistening effects last only about five minutes. Thicker oils, petroleum jelly, or cold cream work the best. I make my own lotion with a combination of these things. When others use it, their reaction is usually "It's greasy," but it's exactly what I need. When dry skin gets too dry, it can crack and become very painful. So, the more moisture I can add, the better I feel.

Managing my pain and itching has been a constant struggle. I don't like prescription pain medication, so I rely heavily on over-the-counter pain relievers. But managing the severity of the infection requires a hierarchy of medications I can run through, ramping up my strategy to match the severity. First is Neosporin. A tube of Neosporin, more specifically the kind that has the numbing agent in it, is somewhere on my person at all times. My next option is Betadine. You may recognize it as the red iodine-looking stuff they use to disinfect an area before surgery. It can be helpful to dry out oozing or infected sores. And my last-ditch effort to avoid antibiotics is a powder called Domeboro, which is a medication used to draw out infection in burn patients. It requires mixing a powder with warm water and drizzling the liquid onto the cloth over my sore. It never fails that infections occur in places that I cannot reach. My mom and now my husband often have to step up for me. I worry about what I will do when they are not around.

Covering my sores has always been a problem. The trouble with bandages is that they usually will not stick at all because of the oils I put on my skin. And if they do stick to my skin, they pull off my skin when they are removed. Band-Aids only work on my fingers, where they can wrap around and stick to themselves. If I ever have to get an EKG or the doctor wants me to wear a heart monitor, I put up quite a bit of protest. When those round sticky things come off, so does my skin. I try to slowly remove them so as little skin as possible is ripped, but it is inevitable. One time I had a nurse come into my hospital room, grab all the wires at once, and yank them off. I wasn't very happy, and I might have punched her if I could have reached her. And if I ever have an IV, I get the nurses to let me remove the sticky stuff that holds it in place.

My point is that my wounds are most often open and uncovered. Many times I have had to miss work because I had a sore in a location that would not allow me to wear clothes. I get very angry when my skin gets in the way of my daily life.

Medication and Side Effects

At the beginning of my school-age years, my parents were told about a new medication. It was being developed but wasn't approved in the United States yet. Somehow, they were able to get it from Europe. I will never forget the day it arrived at my house. By this point, my dermatologist was my dad's best friend. He came over to my house with this giant wrapped present. My parents helped me open it to find another wrapped box and another wrapped box and another. I don't remember how many boxes there were, but I do remember that everyone was watching me and laughing. At some point, I got so overwhelmed that I started crying and wouldn't open any more boxes. I am sure I was expecting some type of present and didn't consider medication to be a present.

This medication did improve my quality of life some. But though it made the thick scales lessen, it also made my skin thinner—an improvement in appearance but more blisters and potential for injuries. The risks were considerable. My doctor was most concerned about the potential for kidney and liver damage. There was a danger of extra bone growth in the form of bone spurs as well. I went every six months for bloodwork and every year for x-rays. Because of ichthyosis, my veins seem to be very hard to find. To this day, any time I get bloodwork done or need an IV, I say lots of prayers. Frequently, the emergency rooms send for an ultrasound machine to help find a vein.

Although my kidney and liver remain unaffected by the medication, I do have trouble with my cholesterol and triglycerides. But I manage these issues with diet and another medication. The medication for my skin is believed to be so hard on my body that my doctor took me off it during the summer of my sixteenth year. He said it would "give my body a break." I remember having to take pain medication and antidepressant medications in its place. I developed hard, painful welts and had lots of infections. The depression that came with returning to my pre-medicine skin was difficult. It was not my favorite summer.

The most critical side effect was the high potential (25 percent) for severe birth defects in my future children that included heart defects, eye/ear/facial abnormalities, cleft palate, heart defects, hydrocephalus, unusually small head, intellectual disabilities, and central nervous system malformations. The potential problems are considered so severe that anyone on the medication is required to be on two types of birth control. This, of course, did not apply to me because I was a child. I remember my parents talking to me about the possible birth defects and the strong possibility that I would not be able to have children. Not that I *couldn't*, but that I *shouldn't*. I was a child and didn't care. None of the dangers or side effects mattered. If it made my life better, I was ready to try it.

The medication was approved in the US within a few years and was replaced with a slightly less harmful medication a few years later. I am still on this medication today, and I am tested regularly for issues with my kidneys, liver, and bones. As I approach age fifty, I am blessed to say that I have been free of any serious side effects. I do have some annoying minor side effects such as chapped lips, fingertips that peel, dry eyes, and curly hair. They told me that the medication might make my hair fall out, so I will not complain about the curls. Curly hair is better than no hair. And compared to life before the medication, it is well worth it.

When I talk about this medication on social media, I get quite a bit of angry feedback from other ichthyosis patients who have tried it. Many are very passionate when they warn me about how much it has ruined their life with horrible side effects. They describe lots of pain related to skeletal complications and other issues. I am thankful for my experience thus far and continue to take it knowing the risk for potential problems. When I informed my doctor that I would physically fight him or take him to court if he threatened to take me off my medication again, he just chuckles. I'm pretty sure he thinks I'm kidding. It is because of this medication that I can live a semi-normal life, and I cannot imagine life without it.

I hope I have done a decent job of explaining the physical challenges of my disease. Now I want to share with you some stories about how it has affected me socially. As you might imagine, I was aware of my differences, and my differences were noticeable to others. God created us as social beings, and I had a disease that others did not understand. It is because of my social struggles that I developed some very skewed views of myself. But these struggles are the reason my victory is so powerful.

2

The Social Factor

To sum up, all of you be harmonious, sympathetic, brotherly, kindhearted, and humble in spirit; not returning evil for evil or insult for insult, but giving a blessing instead; for you were called for the very purpose that you might inherit a blessing.

– 1 Peter 3:8–9 (NASB)

Right now, you may be saying to yourself, *What does all of this have to do with me? I don't have a skin disease.* Well, if you have ever felt different or been teased or had trouble making friends, hang tight. I want to talk to you about how my social life, identity, and beliefs about myself were affected by ichthyosis.

The truth is, we all experience pain, and I hope that somehow what I have learned from my pain can help you with yours. We can be greatly impacted by our experiences as a child, and while I was safe and loved at home, the world was a scary place. Ultimately, I had to begin making my own place in it.

Being Different

This next part of my book involves stories I have shared with only a handful of people—some to no one at all. They are not comfortable for me to share and probably won't be comfortable for you to read, but I suspect that most of you will be able to relate to some part of it.

The truth is I was different.

I looked different.

I smelled different.

I dressed different.

The feelings of embarrassment, shame, and fear that I experienced are not unique to me. Millions of people struggle daily with low self-esteem, poor social skills, and social anxiety. I had trouble making friends, starting conversations, and facing the anxiety that accompanied social events. In my mind, everyone was looking at me. In my mind, my skin *was* me.

Whether you feel different because of your skin color, your size, a disability, or some other issue, you are not alone. Some of us don't like our hair or our nose or the size of our feet. For me, what I didn't like about myself happened to be the most visible part of my body. Although it probably wasn't as noticeable as I perceived it to be, that is irrelevant. My perception was my reality. And as you will soon see, this took a toll on my self-esteem and created some painful memories.

Elementary School: Stay Away from Me!

People were bringing little children to Jesus for him to place his hands on them, but the disciples rebuked them. When Jesus saw this, he was indignant. He said to them, "Let the little children come to me, and do not hinder them, for the kingdom of God belongs to such as these. Truly I tell you, anyone who will not

receive the kingdom of God like a little child will never enter it."
And he took the children in his arms, placed his hands on them
and blessed them.

– Mark 10:13–16 (NIV)

My grandmother told me of the time she walked me to Sunday school. Being probably four or five years old, I clung to her, not wanting her to leave. She let me sit in her lap and watch the other children play until I found the courage to join them. When I finally decided to play, I went over to a table that had puzzles and playdough on it. Within a couple of minutes, another child came over to the same table, but as soon as she saw my thick, scaly hands, she asked, "What's wrong with your hands?" My grandmother says that I shrunk back into her lap and didn't venture away again.

My earliest childhood memory was my first day of first grade. I have seen pictures of earlier events but don't remember any of them. I used to be shocked that I cannot remember a good bit of my childhood. I have since learned that the trauma associated with a painful childhood illness hijacked my memory. My body and brain were focused on getting through the day, not on remembering what was happening.

On the first day of first grade, I remember a little boy in my class pitching a screaming fit because I was in his class. I remember him screaming, "But I don't wanna be in her class!" He was crying real tears and was genuinely scared that he had to be close to me. The teacher tried to calm him, but nothing she did seemed to be working. To my six-year-old brain, this seemed to go on for several minutes. I could feel all the children watching the scene with uncomfortable, wide-eyed stares. I don't think the teacher knew what to say or do. I remember sitting very still, looking at my desk and keeping my head down. I have no idea how it ended or whether that boy even remained in my class. I just wanted it over. I wanted to disappear.

The comments I heard from other kids in elementary school included the following:

"You are gross!"

"You stink!"

"Doesn't your mother ever bathe you?"

"I don't want to sit by her!"

"You can't sit here!"

"What's wrong with your skin?"

"Your skin looks like dried playdough!"

I heard these comments often. Sometimes daily. I heard them in the classroom, at lunch, on the bus, and regularly during playtime. I can remember times when we were asked to do some type of circle activity that involved holding hands in PE. The other kids would nervously jockey for position so that they weren't the one having to stand by me. I would hold out my hand, and they would awkwardly look from my face to my hand. Then they would hold on to my sleeve so they didn't have to touch me.

When we played Red Rover, I tried to get on the end so only one person had to hold my hand. But that kid and I were always a target because the other team knew I would jerk my hand away at the last second—I had to let the other team's player run through, or else I would have the skin ripped off my arm or hand. I often wonder why any teacher would have even asked me to play such a game. Today we are so quick to provide kids with excuses to get out of doing things they don't want to do. If ever there was a reason not to play Red Rover, I had one.

I did have a couple of faithful friends in elementary school that would sit with me on the bus. If a kid said something about me being gross or stinky, they would respond by saying, "She doesn't stink!" and then lean over to take a big whiff, as if doing so could prove my tormentors wrong. I had a couple of friends who I had sleepovers with, and I was invited to the occasional birthday party. But I was always shy, taking in everything from the sidelines and trying not to draw attention to myself.

My oldest friend is someone who I have known since birth. We would spend a week at each other's house each summer and write letters regularly when apart. (I love telling my students about snail mail. They find it amazing that we had to wait days to get a message to each other.) She is much shorter than I but is feisty with her protective nature. She tells stories about when kids would see us out shopping together. They would freeze and stare at me, every single time, and it would make her so angry.

We were eleven years old when the World's Fair came to Knoxville, Tennessee, in 1982. As we stood in line for an exhibit, my friend noticed an adult staring at my legs. She turned around with her hands on her hips and said, "What are you looking at?" We were completely comfortable around each other, and she always treated me as if I was just like anyone else. She would even, in secret, peel my skin with tweezers. She is the reason I know I am not the only one who loves to peel skin.

Pretend That They Are Invisible and I Am Deaf

> *For You have been a strong-place for those who could not help themselves and for those in need because of much trouble. You have been a safe place from the storm and a shadow from the heat.*
>
> *– Isaiah 25:4*

Throughout my childhood, comments and stares from other children and even some adults were a daily part of my life. Many people were afraid to touch me, and most didn't want to be close to me. I saw their reactions and heard their comments. But I had to find a way to get through my days despite it all. There was no cure for my disease, and I couldn't live in a bubble. I had to learn to cope with the comments and stares as best I could. The way I saw it, I had four choices:

Option 1—I could go home and tell my parents what was happening, but that was never my style. For one thing, I didn't want to tell my parents because it was embarrassing to talk about. Revealing to them what happened meant having to relive it, and that was hard. The other reason I didn't tell my parents was because I didn't want any more attention drawn to me. I didn't want my mom going to the school and complaining. I saw it as something I had to deal with, something they couldn't protect me from. My mom always told me that others just didn't understand. And she was right. They didn't understand what was wrong with me or how to handle their feelings when they looked at me. I didn't really blame them.

I am sure my parents knew I was being teased and wanted to protect me. But I couldn't bring myself to upset them by telling them every time someone commented on the way I looked or smelled. My parents did everything they could to create a safe and loving home, but they couldn't shelter me from the world. I just wasn't the type to run home and tell my mommy that someone was mean to me at school. I accepted it as a part of my reality and kept it to myself.

Option 2—I could tell the teacher, but what would that do? It would probably make me a bigger target. The kids weren't going to stop, and they never teased me when teachers could hear. I believe that some of the teachers were grossed out by me too; they just couldn't say it. Besides, snitching on them meant having to admit it was happening. It meant facing hurt, shame, and embarrassment, three feelings I have spent a lifetime trying to avoid.

I often hear stories in the news about students being bullied at school and teachers allegedly "doing nothing about it." I refuse to believe these reports because every educator I know *will* step in when they see a child being teased or bullied. Kids are sneaky, but if a teacher sees it, it will be addressed. Furthermore, when a teacher does address an issue, it is done in private. How the school disciplines a child is not divulged to the class or reported to other parents. Just because the results are not announced over the intercom or posted in the media does not mean that it is not being addressed.

The consequences schools are allowed to issue when students are bullied is a matter as well. We can take privileges, assign chores or extra work, require apologies, call home, and suspend and sometimes expel a student. What we cannot do is prevent a student from speaking. As I said earlier, teasing usually happens out of teacher earshot. It is a tough issue for everyone, and I don't have all the answers. As a school counselor, I teach many lessons on feelings, social skills, and empathy. I try to teach the children at my school to put themselves in someone else's shoes and to treat others with compassion.

Option 3—I could stand up for myself. Well, let me just say, I did what I could. Since everyone was afraid of catching my disease or didn't want to touch me, the incidents never got physical. I did try saying, "No, I'm not!" to comments about me being gross or "Nuh uh" when kids said I stunk. But honestly, I was shy and quiet, and I knew they were right. My skin *was* gross, and it *did* smell!

Option 4—I could just not react at all. Ignore them. *Pretend that they were invisible and I was deaf.* This option seemed to work the best for me. I don't think my choice to ignore them was a conscious decision, but it was the best thing I could do to get through the day. If I could pretend the teasing wasn't happening, the bell would eventually ring, and I could go back home to my safe place. So, I pretended that they were invisible and I was deaf.

Ignoring what was happening became a coping mechanism for me that has followed me throughout my life. I can remember standing at the front of the bus, waiting to get off at my driveway. The kids sitting near the front were saying ugly things to me as the bus came to a stop. As soon as the doors opened, I got off the bus and pretended it didn't happen. I knew that it would happen again the next day, but that didn't matter. No one would put me down or make fun of me until the next morning when school began again. I was home, and I was safe.

I've studied about the ways other people cope with painful and threatening situations and have learned that I am not alone in my response. The child who is abused pretends it isn't happening in the moment and then tries to forget about it. I know people who did such a good job of forgetting about it that they literally forgot about it. It is a common survival skill. The event is too painful to process at the time, so it is shoved somewhere in the recesses of the mind. Of course, at some point, the memories resurface and must be dealt with. Usually this happens later in life when the person is more cognitively equipped to deal with what happened to them.

I have to give credit to my parents because staying home from school or giving up was never an option. Feeling sorry for myself wasn't an option either. It never entered my mind. I went to school, did my work and did what I had to do to get by. Don't get me wrong, it hurt. Physically and emotionally. I was embarrassed and ashamed at the things that were happening to me. It absolutely affected the way I thought about myself. It wasn't until many years later that I would be able to deal with those thoughts and feelings, but I will get to that later.

Teen Years

> *It is the LORD who goes before you. He will be with you; he will not leave you or forsake you. Do not fear or be dismayed.*
>
> *– Deuteronomy 31:8 (ESV)*

Secondary school was more of the same. The kids weren't as bold as in elementary school, and they rarely said anything to my face. But I heard the comments and noticed when the crowd in the hallways parted because I was walking by.

You stink.

I don't wanna sit by her.

I maintained the same method that had worked for me in grammar school: I pretended that they were invisible and I was deaf. I would look down or straight ahead and keep walking.

I attended an all-girls school that required us to wear short-sleeve dresses. This meant I could not cover my legs, which were thick, scaly, and often covered with sores. I would wear one sweater over my dress to cover my arms and carry another sweater to cover my legs in class. I would, of course, do this even when it was hot outside, and if anyone asked, I would always say I was cold. But they hardly ever asked because they didn't want to look at my skin either.

I had a couple of friends in middle and high school but didn't hang out with them outside of school. I was a good student, and despite my issues, I liked going to school. Still, I tried to do anything I could not to get noticed. Undoubtedly, the things I was attempting to ignore were happening, even though I tried to leave it all behind at the end of every day and act as if I wasn't bothered by any of it. I can see in retrospect how much grit and resilience I demonstrated on a daily basis. Isn't that what we do? We suck it up, look straight ahead, and keep going.

The young lady whose locker was always next to mine was in an unfortunate spot. For six years she had to share space with me at our lockers. And since most teachers seated us in alphabetical order, she had to be close to me in class too. I remember her pitching small fits about it on occasions. One time she said, "Why do I always have to sit by her?" If we were at our lockers at the same time, she would say, "Ew," and step way back until I was gone. I would look at her apologetically, sometimes even apologizing out loud. If she was there first, I would wait until she was gone to get what I needed. I don't really blame her; nevertheless, it did hurt. Of course, I pretended that she was invisible and I was deaf. I pretended I didn't hear her complaints nor notice her wrinkle her nose. I pretended none of it was happening. I hold no resentment toward her—I would not have wanted to be beside me either.

In junior high, we were required to perform a dance for our parents during some type of recital. Our costumes consisted of the typical leotards. I was self-conscious about having bare legs, so my mother asked for special permission for me to wear tights under my leotard. Although they agreed, they were upset that I was ruining the continuity of the group. They emphasized that I would be the *only* one who was wearing tights and would stand out. But I would rather stand out and be covered than stand out and be seen.

The fact that I agreed to dance in the first place astonishes me now. Maybe my parents didn't give me a choice. As I said, I don't remember quitting ever being an option. My mother sometimes questions whether she made the right decisions in these types of circumstances. I emphatically say that she did. She taught me not to give up and not to use my skin as an excuse, which I honestly never did. I sometimes had a reason not to do something because of my skin but never an excuse. To me, there is a difference.

Another memory I have is of a dance class in high school when the teacher sat us all down on the floor to have a talk. She began to lecture us about the importance of bathing and wearing deodorant. She mentioned how inappropriate it was to use scented lotions or perfume as a substitute for bathing. Of course, I *did* bathe—daily! I was aware of the odor of my skin, and I did do what I could to manage it. I also strove to do everyone a favor by sitting a good distance away from them whenever possible. But that day, *everyone* sitting on the floor knew her speech was directed at me. It got very quiet. No one looked at me, and I looked at the floor, pretending she was invisible and I was deaf. The shame and embarrassment I felt were difficult to bear. But again, I told no one.

I believe that teacher has passed away, and I hold no resentment toward her. But she handled it all wrong. As a school counselor, I have had teachers come to me with complaints about stinky students. I usually start with calling home and explaining that I am concerned about the potential for other children to start bullying this student. I ask the parents if there is anything I can do to help. Sometimes parents will tell me that the child won't bathe when told to do so. Other times, the parent isn't aware that maybe it is time for their child to be using deodorant. It is only after this conversation with the parent that I might talk with the student, and I would never do it in front of the whole class. If my teacher had called my mom to talk about the issue, my mom would have educated her on my disease and helped her to be more compassionate. That incident is a scar on my heart that still hurts on occasion.

I am not sure if it was my sophomore or junior year when I took a Bible class. At some point during the semester, we were asked to write a paper. I cannot remember what the paper was about, but I do remember that it was anonymous. When writing this paper, I admitted for the first time that I had thoughts of suicide. I only mentioned it briefly and didn't give it much thought. I guess I felt safe to be honest. About three weeks later, my Bible teacher came to me and said that she had used my handwriting to narrow down the author of that paper to me. Then she asked me about my comments in the paper related to suicide. I remember feeling two things: panic and gratitude. My immediate response to her was to lie. *No, I didn't really have those thoughts anymore. Maybe I had them in the past but not anymore.* The truth was that I didn't want anyone to tell my parents what I had written. And I don't think she did. But I also felt immense gratitude. Someone was listening. Someone noticed. And that meant a lot.

As I grew up and tried different treatments, I got better at managing my symptoms but was still in a good deal of pain by the end of most days at school. We weren't allowed to wear sandals to school and Crocs weren't around back then. I don't recall what shoes I wore, but I do remember the many blisters on my feet. At some point during my high school years, we tried baby oil instead of cold cream on my skin, and that seemed to lessen the odor. My medication was making my skin less thick and scaly while at the same time making it extra thin and more injury prone. I tended to scratch and claw myself in my sleep, so I frequently had large sores on my arms and legs, which I tried to hide. During my senior year, I had to stand in front of the whole school and give a speech. On that day, I also had a palm-sized sore on the back of my calf, so I pushed through and did what I had to do, all the while pretending the sore wasn't there.

Throughout high school, obviously, I didn't date. No one showed any interest. I didn't participate in sports, and I wasn't involved in any extracurricular activities. I attended my junior prom with a male friend from church and my senior prom with two of my female friends. I knew that if other girls didn't want to be near me, there was no chance a boy would ever notice me. It was what it was, and I accepted it. I assumed that I would be alone forever. Why would any guy want to love me? That was a thought that would stay with me for a long time.

My local Methodist church had been my church home my entire life. It was the place where I found the most friends during my teenage years. We went to church every Sunday and Wednesday, and I was an active member of my youth group. When I was at church, I had friends who accepted me. They chose to sit by me, to room with me on retreats, and hang out with me outside of church. To this day my best friend is a lady I met at church when we were ten years old. She has been there for me in so many ways. She has loved me despite my skin and my bad habits—and I definitely had some bad habits.

I do feel honored by something special that happened my sophomore year of high school. My fellow classmates voted for me to receive an award, which recognized me for courage and determination. It meant the world to me that they recognized how difficult it was for me to even show up at school every day. They might not have wanted to be near me or be friends with me, but they recognized my struggle and respected my perseverance. I do not harbor any anger or resentment toward any of these girls. I understood their reaction and often felt the need to apologize for my own presence.

Home

Love the LORD your God with all your heart and with all your soul and with all your strength. These commandments that I give you today are to be on your hearts. Impress them on your children. Talk about them when you sit at home and when you walk along the road, when you lie down and when you get up.

– Deuteronomy 6:5–7 (NIV)

Home consisted of my parents, my two older sisters, and me. Although home wasn't perfect, I was accepted, loved, and safe. My parents took me to a psychiatrist for an evaluation when I was young and were told to raise me as if I were normal. Of course, there were exceptions, but for the most part, I was expected to keep up. I know there were times when my sisters protested because I wasn't asked to do certain chores that they were asked to do, usually because it would hurt me or make me too hot. But generally, I was treated just like my sisters. I pulled weeds, cleaned my room, did the dishes, and mowed the grass. My mom would try to find chores for me inside when the weather was too hot.

My dad believed in exposing us to different cultures, so we traveled a couple of times a year. My parents always thought ahead and made sure that the activities we were going to do were suitable for me. I always knew that as long as they were there someone had my back, like understanding I had to walk slower because of blisters or my need to get out of the heat. If they were around, I knew I could say the word and they would move mountains to get me cool. My mother would even wear my new shoes for a couple of weeks so they didn't hurt me as much when I began to wear them.

I am very blessed by the opportunities I have had to travel, and I am so thankful for the adventures. Cruises work very well for me, especially destinations to cold locations. Alaska is my favorite. A much-loved vacation was when I went snowmobiling with my parents and my husband for a week. Since Greg is in a wheelchair, we usually have an imbalance— something he can't do that I can and vice versa. But on a snowmobile, we are equal. On a snowmobile, it is game on. My skin was safe from injury under the big fluffy snowsuit, and Greg's handicap disappeared on a snowmobile. We had a blast! Greg even went to Hardees on his snowmobile and brought me a biscuit. I still crave adventures with him, although they are getting less frequent.

A couple of years ago, my mom, Greg, and I went to Washington DC. To limit my steps and my exposure to the heat, we took a taxi everywhere we went. We didn't ever walk more than a couple of blocks, especially if it was above eighty degrees. Because Greg is wheelchair bound, we had to order special taxis that could accommodate his electric chair. One day we visited the United States Capitol and spent a couple of hours touring there. Then we walked to the National Botanical Gardens, which was within sight of the Capitol Building.

What might seem like a short distance to some had the potential to be a problem for me. Limiting steps is critical, but the walk didn't seem that far. The temperature was rising, and I got a little too warm on the walk. The sun was blazing, and the temperature in the shade was a few degrees less, so I took an even longer route to stay in the shade, something I often do. As soon as we stepped inside the air conditioning, we sat for a while to let my body cool off. But after about fifteen minutes, the fire alarm went off, and we were required to exit the building, back into the heat. I quickly went from being a little too warm to overly hot, and if I didn't get help soon, I would have had a problem.

I couldn't walk back up the hill to the Capitol Building without getting hotter. There were no taxis around, much less ones that could accommodate Greg's wheelchair. My seventy-two-year-old mom ended up chasing down a tour bus that had a handicapped symbol on the side. She basically got on and refused to get off. The bus driver explained to her that we had to buy tickets for his tour bus at some other location. She handed him some money and explained to him that he *was* going to let us on and that he *was* going to get my husband's wheelchair on that bus. My point is, I know that my family gets it. They listen to me and act quickly when I need them. At forty-nine years old, I am still hesitant to go anywhere without one of them. My fear is that others will ignore my needs or not take them seriously.

My sisters have always been protective of me too. One time in first grade, our school bus broke down on a hot day. Both of my sisters used their books to fan me in an effort to keep me cool. My family has gotten ice to put on my neck when I'm hot and walked super slow so that my feet wouldn't blister. They've helped me wrap my legs with sheets of protective gel so that I could snow ski. They've dropped me off at the door to the mall so that I could save a few steps. It was a constant battle, and they were willing to try anything to help. They've protected me any way they could, but they couldn't be with me all the time. They couldn't protect me from the world, nor could they fight all my battles for me.

Lost

But you, LORD, are a compassionate and gracious God, slow to anger, abounding in love and faithfulness.

— Psalm 86:15

Then Jesus told them this parable: "Suppose one of you has a hundred sheep and loses one of them. Doesn't he leave the ninety-nine in the open country and go after the lost sheep until he finds it? And when he finds it, he joyfully puts it on his shoulders and goes home. Then he calls his friends and neighbors together and says, "Rejoice with me; I have found my lost sheep."

— Luke 15:3–6

For I know the thoughts that I think toward you, says the Lord, thoughts of peace and not of evil, to give you a future and a hope.

— Jeremiah 29:11 (NKJV)

As I grew up and entered adulthood, something was starting to happen in my soul, in the core of my being. I didn't recognize it yet, but I was developing some very unhealthy core beliefs about myself. Deep in my heart, in a place that I didn't even realize was there, I was convinced that I was *unlovable, unwanted,* and *defective.* To be honest, there has always been a part of me that felt the need to apologize for my presence. I don't want to make other people feel uncomfortable or gross them out. If I had to ask for help or special treatment because of my skin, I made an apology. If I left skin on someone's dark-colored couch or black clothing, I would say I was sorry. Outside of the safety of my home, I was someone who was tolerated—but not wanted.

As you read in Chapter 2, I was a person other people did not seek out. In fact, most made it clear that they were uncomfortable around me. I was different and stinky and gross. And from the day I was born, most people outside of my family didn't want to touch me or be near me. My appearance disturbed them, and I felt the need to apologize often. As a result of my skin condition, I didn't have many opportunities to make friends. I avoided most social situations except for church and tried to fly under the radar as much as possible. Most days, my goal was to avoid getting noticed. I was safe at home, but out in the world, I felt like an outcast.

The problem was that I did exist. I had to go to school and work. I still needed to find a way to live in this world. While I never wanted attention because of my skin, I did crave attention in general. I wanted to be normal and noticed and loved and desired. If you are familiar with Maslow's hierarchy of needs, you know that a sense of belonging is an important part of what we need to be happy and content. People who experience loneliness and do not feel accepted by a social group are much more likely to have health problems as well as problems with depression and anxiety. We *need* a sense of connection with others. I am not proud of what I am about to share with you, but what I did came from a place of hurt and shame. It is embarrassing, but I share it with you because I think many of you will be able to relate.

Playing the Victim

Although I wasn't conscious of it at the time, I began lying to get attention. There, I said it. I know I am not the only person to have ever done this, but it is not something I am proud of. And although I am embarrassed by what I did, I understand it for what it was—the actions of a hurting and lonely child who desired to be loved. I see it often in the elementary school students I work with. They will make up wild and crazy stories to get a reaction from their peers. They lie about things they don't need to lie about and can get quite creative in defending their lies. I have had children talk to me about siblings they don't have or deaths that never occurred. One kid insisted that he caught a shark in the Tennessee River. Some kids get so good at telling these stories they begin to believe them. It can be a difficult habit to overcome. They don't believe that they are good enough or interesting enough to warrant attention and love from others, so they lie to draw people closer to them.

This habit of lying became especially prominent in my life when I went off to college and tried to make friends. Instead of living in a dorm, I shared an apartment with my sister. Making friends was difficult. Because I wasn't in a dorm and didn't participate in any extracurricular activities, I had to go in search of friends. It seemed like no one wanted to be around me, and I didn't know how to connect with them. But if I had a problem or was upset, I could at least get others to notice me. So I fabricated or exaggerated problems that kept people coming to check on me. I discovered that people in a church setting were especially prone to help even the most unlovable person. And since I wasn't very good at making friends and didn't feel lovable, this became a big part of the way I worked: I got my need for love and attention met by not being OK. In fact, I got so good at acting like I was not OK that I started to really *not* be OK. Being a victim became part of who I was for a while.

It was the beginning of a bad and embarrassing habit. I'd pretend to be upset and would feign crying or even lie to keep people in my life. I think my church friends realized that I was insecure and afraid, so they played along and loved me anyway. Without realizing it, I was doing what worked—though it did backfire sometimes, when a few friends got tired of the attention-getting tactics and didn't hang around very long. When I would sense people withdrawing, I would increase my efforts to draw them back in with some sort of lie. This, of course, sent them running. I do want to make it clear that I *never* lied about my skin issues or used it to get attention. In fact, I would lie to cover up my skin or my limitations rather than let others see it.

Although it wasn't easy, I can say that this is a habit I have overcome. Getting a job and getting married helped curb some of the fear of being alone and gave me a bigger social group. My job helped meet some of my social needs. I had people to talk to and interact with daily, which eased the isolation I had felt for so many years. Once I met my husband and saw that he wanted to be close to me, I no longer needed to lie to get attention. I was accepted by his family, and he became my safe haven. It helped that he was such an outgoing guy and made friends everywhere we went. I often tell people that my husband could talk to a wall. As long as I had him, I was OK. He met my need of feeling loved and belonging.

More Bad Habits

I do not understand what I do. For what I want to do I do not do, but what I hate I do. And if I do what I do not want to do, I agree that the law is good. As it is, it is no longer I myself who do it, but it is sin living in me. For I know that good itself does not dwell in me, that is, in my sinful nature. For I have the desire to do what is good, but I cannot carry it out. For I do not do the good I want to do, but the evil I do not want to do—this I keep doing.

– Romans 7:15–19

In college I started out as a psychology major with a pre-med focus. I had planned to go to medical school. I am not sure where this idea came from, but realistically speaking, it was a ludicrous idea. I couldn't walk or stand for more than a couple of hours without getting blisters, so how would I have gotten through twenty-four-hour shifts in medical school? Fortunately, God had other plans for me, and I didn't get into medical school but went on to get a master's degree in community agency counseling. I always had a desire to help others who have been through tough times, so it seemed natural that I head in the direction of counseling. I remember a poem I wrote in junior high about why bad things happen to people. I was never able to find the answer, except that we all suffer and need each other to get through this broken world. Surely there were others out there like me who I could help.

With a master's degree in counseling, my first job out of college was as an alcohol and drug counselor. It was tiring, draining, and thankless. "I need to go to rehab, Mom!" said no kid ever. My clients were angry, did not want help, and had an addiction that made them miserable. Almost every teen who came to us smoked cigarettes along with the other drugs they used, and since it is illegal for kids to smoke, we had to take that away from them too. They were almost always forced to be there, either by their parents or by the court system. Some of them tried to run away, and most expressed anger toward the staff. We tried not to take it personally, but it was difficult. Holidays were the hardest because rehabs never close. During times when others in the world were celebrating, I was working with angry, addicted teenagers. Their angry attitudes and foul language seeped into my daily life, and I picked up on some of their bad habits.

First, I cussed—a lot! Since teenagers in rehab used lots of curse words, I justified my bad language by telling myself I had to talk that way to relate to them. This language followed me home and became something I did regularly. It took concentration not to slip in front of my family or around little children, but somehow, I managed. I am thankful that I am slowly winning the battle to remove these words from my vocabulary, but it hasn't been easy.

Second, I became a smoker. Most of the people who work in a rehab are recovering addicts themselves. It is their way of keeping themselves in contact with the fragility of their own addiction. Most of them still cling to their less harmful addictions to caffeine and nicotine. Smoke breaks and coffee were constant occurrences. While I never liked coffee, I did become a smoker. If I was going to relate to my coworkers, I had to be there for conversations, all of which happened on smoke breaks.

This was, of course, back before there were such strict rules about smoking. We never smoked inside, but a group of us usually gathered outside to smoke. If I didn't join them, I'd miss out on those bonding moments, yet it never dawned on me to go out with them and *not* smoke. Before I knew it, I was smoking a pack a day. I am happy to admit that, after fifteen years, I finally quit smoking. I often tell people that it was the hardest thing I have ever done. Giving up cigarettes was much harder than watching my dad die. If you are ever tempted to smoke, don't. Just don't. It isn't worth it. You don't get a prize or a sticker or an apple at the end of the day for doing it. It doesn't make you cool, and the negative consequences are no secret.

Lastly, if you work in an alcohol and drug rehab, the clients and staff will respect you more when you are a recovering addict. Pretty much everyone who worked where I did had "been there, done that." But I wasn't in recovery. In fact, I had never done drugs at all. But to gain credibility with my coworkers and the patients, I decided it was important to act as if I was a recovering addict. If you weren't a recovering addict, you weren't in the club—at least that is how it felt. Continuing my pattern of lying, I pretended to be in recovery. I was so good at lying by now that they never had a clue.

After a few years of working at the rehab, I had a coworker come to me with concerns she said had been expressed by other staff members. I felt sorry for her because I'm sure she must have drawn the short straw, and I could tell it was difficult for her. She told me that several staff members were uncomfortable with the skin that fell out of my clothes onto the floor when I went to the restroom. In fact, they were so bothered by it that management would be installing a mini vacuum on the wall in the bathroom so I could vacuum up the skin that fell on the floor. She also told me some coworkers had seen me picking at my skin and were grossed out by that as well. I fought back tears and nodded my head as she talked.

As soon as she left my office, I cried tears of embarrassment and humiliation. I will never forget it. My stomach was in a knot, and my heart was crushed. These were people I interacted with every day, people who I considered my friends. After I was done crying, I—you guessed it—pretended my coworkers were invisible and I was deaf. It was all I knew to do. I tried to pretend it didn't happen and stayed in my office a whole lot more. You may wonder if I ever used that vacuum. Nope, I couldn't do it. It made a fair amount of noise, and it felt like a loudspeaker announcing that I was in the bathroom. I'm sure it wasn't as loud as I considered it to be, but it never got used.

Yet again, my presence made others uncomfortable. I was being asked to remove any evidence that I had been there. It would have been great if I had been able to respond with a more mature attitude and say, "No problem. I totally understand. I will gladly do that for you guys!" But I couldn't. I was so broken inside and ashamed of my disease, this felt like yet another kick in the gut.

My Biggest Regret

The Lord our God is merciful and forgiving, even though we have rebelled against him.

– Daniel 9:9

He has not dealt with us according to our sins, nor punished us according to our iniquities. For as the heavens are high above the earth, so great is His mercy toward those who fear Him; as far as the east is from the west, so far has He removed our transgressions from us.

– Psalm 103: 10–12 (NKJV)

The best thing that came out of my job as an alcohol and drug counselor was my husband, Greg. He worked there as the teacher and was the first person I met when I walked in the building. He gave me a tour of the building, showed me where everything was, and treated me with genuine kindness. We love it when people ask us how we met. We can honestly tell them that "we met in rehab." It's so fun to watch them stammer and stutter!

Although work was difficult, Greg and I became close friends. He seemed to accept me for who I was, enjoyed my company, and was interested in learning about my disease. He never said anything negative about my skin or my smell. He was very angry when that whole vacuum incident happened too. We seemed to laugh a lot and enjoyed each other's company. We found ourselves spending an increasing amount of time together. We went to movies and out to eat, played badminton in the gym at work, and even went to local plays.

Greg and I spent five years being friends. He had lost many people in his life shortly before we met, and he told me he wasn't interested in getting married. He would show me pictures of girls he had dated. When I asked him about them, his response was always the same: "She wanted to marry me, but I didn't want to." To top it off, he was eighteen years older than me. Yes, you read that right. I was born the year he graduated high school. Age is just a number, right?

Although we worked together, Greg lived an hour away and often spent nights on my couch. We were both surprised by our continued and increasing desire to be together. We liked being together and, in fact, we craved it. After five years of friendship and eventual dating, I finally reeled him in. He had told me all along that he would have to run sooner or later, just like he had done with every other girl he dated. Yet he kept staying and staying and staying. In fact, he kept leaving more and more of his belongings at my house. I finally convinced him that we were made for each other, and we got married. But shortly before that, something terrible happened.

Remember the doctors telling me about the potential birth defects caused by my skin medication? Remember the warning *not* to ever get pregnant? Well, I got pregnant. And no, we weren't married yet. I considered lying and saying the pregnancy happened after we were married, but I'm trying to be as real as possible. We were sinning, and we paid the consequences. Isn't that the way it works? While it is difficult to share with you, I know that sin is sin, and we are not the only couple to have made this mistake. At twenty-six years old, I found myself engaged, living with my fiancé, and pregnant. It was not my finest hour.

I went to my regular gynecologist and talked to him about the pregnancy. He begged me to consider all my options, especially keeping the baby. He referred me to an at-risk pregnancy doctor who confirmed the high chance of massive birth defects. It wasn't a small chance, like 2 or 3 percent. Nor was it even 10 percent. It was more like a 25 percent chance of severe birth defects. This doctor told me he had an experimental procedure using ulcer medication that might induce a miscarriage. I was forty-two days along, and he had only been successful with the procedure up to forty-four days. With only two days to discuss it, Greg and I decided to terminate the pregnancy.

This decision is one of the biggest regrets of my life and a huge part of my story. I told myself for years that I did the right thing because I spared the baby a potentially horrible life. I made lots of excuses and even convinced myself that it was the right thing to do. Wrong! Let me be clear: *It was the wrong decision.* It was a decision I would regret forever. No doubt, I took the cowardly and selfish way out. I never considered what God might have to say about my decision. I never considered that God might be bigger than any medication I was taking.

At the time, I told Greg and one friend, but no one else. It was a very personal and private thing for the two of us. We were adults and felt like it was no one else's business. I know abortion is a controversial topic for many people. Everyone seems to feel strongly about it one way or the other. But to be honest, I'm not interested in anyone else's opinion. Many people try to comfort me or help me justify my decision. But there is no justifying what I did. If you ever find yourself pregnant and unsure what to do, please consider that God is bigger than any obstacle you face. The decision to abort a child will likely cause you a great deal of shame and regret for the rest of your life. Get help. Find out about your options. There are thousands of couples out there who would be happy to adopt your child.

When I found out that I was pregnant, my coping strategy of pretending a certain occurrence wasn't happening took over. By then, I had gotten really good at that. When I was at the doctor, I imagined myself as an actress, playing a role. I pretended that it wasn't happening to me but to someone else. I did what the doctor asked—got a couple of shots and took the medication as directed.

Greg and I took a week off work and waited. The doctor told us that it was unclear when the medication would begin to do its job, so we stayed close to home. I can't remember how we pulled it off because my parents lived right next door. I think we hid our cars at the grocery store down the street each morning and had my best friend bring us back to the house. Somehow, we managed to keep it a secret. We hibernated in my house, played video games, and waited. After a few days, I started to have cramps. It appeared to be working.

I remember going to a checkup where the doctor did an ultrasound to see the progress of the miscarriage. There was a monitor next to me and a monitor on the wall in front of me so I could see it. The monitor next to me made these weird sounds and showed a picture of my uterus. I tried not to look.

The doctor had multiple medical students in the room that day, and he seemed excited to explain his new procedure. As he started talking and calling their attention to various details on the monitor, someone in the room said, "Stop! Can you turn those screens? I don't want to see that!" It was me, of course. But I almost didn't recognize my own voice. He turned off the monitor in front of me and tilted the other one away so I couldn't see it.

He could tell that I was about to lose my composure and awkwardly tried to use quiet hand signals to show his students what was happening on the screen. But at this point I was having trouble with the whole "pretend this isn't happening" thing. He was making it very hard to playact and was invading the fantasy world I had created for myself. I wouldn't—couldn't—let myself think about it.

I went home and resumed hibernating and waiting. The doctor had assured me the procedure was working. Greg was very supportive during this time and stuck to me like glue. The day I went to the bathroom and felt something fall out of my body, I wailed the most primal sobs. Greg held me until I cried myself out. As soon as it was over, we put it behind us and didn't talk about it again. The only tears I cried were the ones on that very last day, the day my baby fell out of my body. Then it was back to pretending it didn't happen.

The Struggle: Depression and Anxiety

But you, LORD, are a shield around me, my glory, the One who lifts my head high. I call out to the LORD, and he answers me from his holy mountain.

– Psalm 3:3–4

I have told you these things, so that in me you may have peace. In this world you will have trouble. But take heart! I have overcome the world.

– John 16:33

As you can imagine, my efforts to convince myself I wasn't affected by what I had done to my child weren't working. I could run from it and pretend it didn't happen, but my heart knew it did. My deeper mind knew it did. I began to feel like I was in a dark cloud all the time, and I found myself weeping on the way to work. I blamed it on the angry, detoxing kids. I was plagued with self-condemnation, which turned to thoughts of hurting myself.

Greg and I decided that I needed to resign and change careers. Eventually, we got married, and I took a couple of years off work to return to graduate school. Quitting work left me with lots of time on my hands, and I spent most of it trying desperately to find happiness. And just like so many others who have felt lost, I looked in all the wrong places.

The first place I looked was to Greg. He was my rock, my hero. We wanted to be together all the time and depended on each other heavily. Greg's mobility issues were increasing, and I assumed the role of taking care of him as much as he took care of me. Whenever I had anxiety attacks, I needed Greg. If I was scared, I needed Greg. If I was lonely, I needed Greg. He was my sanctuary, my safe place, my savior. I didn't realize what was happening at the time, but I was putting Greg on a throne. Since Greg was my source for everything, even the smallest disagreement between us sent me into a tailspin.

Over the next several years, I searched for other things that made me feel good. I made many bad choices, put myself in dangerous situations, and had friendships that led me in the wrong direction. Everything I tried appeared to work for a while, but the happiness was always fleeting. I sinned *a lot*. And although I do not feel led to confess all my sins to you, let me say that none of it got me what I wanted. It looked good and felt good. But in the end, I was not satisfied or happy. I couldn't find peace. Even when things were going good in my life, I still felt like the ground was falling out from underneath me.

After getting a second master's degree, I got a job as a counselor at an elementary school. God placed me in this school for a reason, and over the next fourteen years, a battle for my soul and for my life would transpire. It makes me sad that it took that long, but I had a long way to go. Thankfully, God surrounded me with Christian men and women who loved him deeply. I didn't spend much time with them outside of school, and I'm not sure that I fit in 100 percent, but they accepted and loved me. They were also vigilant prayer warriors. Although they never spoke it outright, I am pretty sure they knew I was lost and prayed for me often.

I was good at my job and brought some fresh ideas to the school. Though I was loved by the children and by my coworkers, I didn't love myself. I also had some erroneous beliefs about myself and God.

As you can imagine, being a school counselor brought its own set of difficulties. Not only did I struggle with loving myself but my job was to help children who were in some very desperate circumstances. Many of the children were faced with issues of neglect, poverty, abuse, and substance abuse. I was often aware that awful things were happening to them but was unable to get them help.

The system for helping abused or neglected children is complicated. While the Department of Children's Services (DCS) does everything they can to keep children safe, they are overwhelmed by the sheer number of kids needing help. There are too few caseworkers, too many children on each of their caseloads, and nowhere near enough foster homes. Time and time again, I saw children slip through the cracks. It is no one's fault. The fact is if they have no absolute proof of abuse or neglect or the children do not admit to what is happening at home, DCS can't do anything. I loved these kids and spent many nights with a pit in my stomach, worrying about what was happening to them.

Over time, my depression escalated to anxiety. I found myself worrying all the time. I worried that the children were not safe, that I wasn't doing enough to help them, and that my coworkers didn't think I was doing enough. I feared that something might happen to my husband or my family and that I wouldn't have anyone to take care of me after my husband was gone. I was anxious about being alone, about taking care of him, and how I would pick up the slack as he got weaker. I even worried about worrying too much.

I had trouble going to sleep at night because I couldn't stop worrying. I talked to my doctor about my difficulty sleeping, and she gave me a prescription for diazepam, which helped shut my brain off at night. I was aware that this medication could be addictive and that I had to guard against this. I also knew that I could build up a tolerance to it, so I only took one on really bad nights. But on those nights, I was extremely thankful to have it.

I continued this pattern of only taking diazepam a few nights a week, and with refills every thirty days, I would end up with a stash of about twenty or thirty of them. When really bad times would come, I would take much more than the recommended dose. I was so desperate to stop the anxiety and fear, I convinced myself that if one diazepam was good, two was better. And then it became three or four. At times, the anxiety got so bad, I would take one every few minutes until I fell asleep.

The hopelessness I felt eventually led to thoughts of hurting myself. I seemed to be guarded or distracted from these thoughts when I was busy working or engaged with my family. Whenever I was alone, thoughts of anger, shame, and helplessness seemed to crowd my mind. Let me make this clear—I did not want to die. I just wanted the pain to stop. I wanted to feel happy. I didn't like who I was, although I couldn't understand why. After all, I was a "good person." By this point, I had toned down my language, quit smoking, and removed some other sin from my life. But any time I was alone or had even the smallest conflict with Greg, a cycle of dark and negative thoughts would begin. I had zero tolerance for my own pain, and my thoughts raced, filled with "what ifs."

I was embarrassed by my pain and got very good at hiding it. My dark thoughts were coming so fast, I was convinced I was going crazy. I even considered checking myself into a mental hospital for a while, but I was afraid of how this would look to my school system and my family. I was honest with Greg about what I felt and what I was doing, and he was as supportive as he could be. But truthfully, he didn't know what to do.

I worked and hung out with my friends and family while pretending all was well. But in my head and in my heart, all was not well. And it was about to get worse.

Grief

Dear friends, do not be surprised at the fiery ordeal that has come on you to test you. . . . But rejoice inasmuch as you participate in

the sufferings of Christ, so that you may be overjoyed when his
glory is revealed.

– 1 Peter 4:12–13

Greg's mom died in 2007 from cancer, which was a blow to both of us. She held a special place in my heart, and I know she had loved me too. She would often refer to me as "my Kathy." My dad became a quadriplegic that same year. We spent months going back and forth between Greg's mom's home in Alabama and the hospital with my dad. I have debated with myself about whether to include my dad's illness in this book, but I think what happened to him significantly contributed to my depression and anxiety, so I decided to tell you the story.

My parents were at a tractor pull in Toledo, Ohio, in August of 2007. My dad had been suffering from a pretty severe cold and had been told by his doctor not to leave town, but not surprisingly, he went anyway. They drove to Ohio with friends, and the night they arrived he began having trouble breathing. I got a call from my mom telling me she was taking him to the emergency room and then another telling me that they were admitting him with double pneumonia. The friends they were traveling with flew home, and Greg and I flew to Toledo to be with my mom.

By the time we arrived, he was in ICU, and they were aggressively treating his pneumonia. He had some other health issues that were complicating things, so when we mentioned to the doctors that his neck was swollen, they didn't seem too concerned. Over the next several days, the swelling in his neck seemed to worsen, so they ran a CT scan but found nothing. They said that he must have pulled a muscle in his neck on the drive to Ohio, and dismissed it (insert eye roll here). They did, however, find that he had methicillin-resistant Staphylococcus aureus (MRSA) in his bloodstream, so they attempted to treat that along with his pneumonia. But as we now know, some MRSA is antibiotic resistant, and apparently, this strand was no exception.

We sought to get him back to Chattanooga via a medically equipped aircraft but had trouble getting a hospital in Chattanooga to accept him because of the MRSA. We knew he and my mom needed to be closer to home. She had already spent a week sleeping in the ICU waiting room. The day that Greg and I left to come home and my sister arrived to take our place in supporting Mom, I was massaging Dad's feet. He was lucid at that moment, and he told me that I was doing it wrong. I thought he was kidding and didn't give it much thought. But by the time we arrived home the next day, he had asked my sister, "Whose feet are those?"

Within a couple days, my mom did successfully get him flown home, where he was admitted into a local hospital. When he told the doctor that he couldn't feel his feet and legs, the doctor admitted to my mom later that his "heart sunk." It turns out that the swelling in his neck was where the MRSA had settled on his spinal column, and it had been pressing on his spine for days. He had walked into the hospital in Ohio but would never walk again. In fact, the paralysis spread up to his neck, and he became a quadriplegic.

During the surgery to try and remove the MRSA pocket off his spine, he nearly died. He came out on a ventilator because his pneumonia was so bad that, combined with his paralysis, he could not breathe on his own. He spent the next four months in ICU on the ventilator. He could not talk or move. He could look at us, and he could cry, but that was pretty much it. My mom and I went to visit him daily, with Mom, naturally, going to see him more often. My sisters and some friends came when they could. We felt powerless to help him, so we did anything we could think of to cheer him up. My nieces and nephew made decorations for the various holidays, and we would hang them all over his ICU room. But still there were times when he would cry so much that his ears filled up with tears.

They told us he might never come off the ventilator, but he eventually did. However, he had to have a tracheotomy. A trach, as it is known, is a hole straight into the person's throat that permits for a tube to be inserted, allowing air to get into their lungs. I had never thought about it before, but if you cannot cough, you cannot get the junk out of your lungs. This was the case with my dad, and he had to have his lungs suctioned out multiple times a day. In late November, they put a special valve over his trach that allowed him to talk, and we heard his voice for the first time in months. We ate Thanksgiving dinner in the hospital, using his bed and body as our table. That is one holiday I will never forget.

He came home in late December, and we set about figuring out how to take care of him. My mom hired caregivers to stay with him, twenty-four hours a day at first. It was not safe to leave him alone, so she needed all the help she could get. We got an electric wheelchair, an electric air bed, and a lift that would pick him up and sit him in the wheelchair. My mom had to learn to manage all his medications as well as how to suction his lungs regularly, change him, dress him, bathe him, and feed him. He could do nothing for himself.

As we adapted to this new normal for our family, we all struggled with watching what was happening to this brilliant, take-charge, proud man we had known. Some days he was lucid and bossing everyone around from the bed. We marveled at how he could have so many of us working on different tasks for him at one time. One day, he waited until my mother left then got his caregiver to order two thousand bulbs out of a flower catalog (I get my love of plants from my dad). My mom then had to figure out what to do with two thousand bulbs! Thankfully, some of them came to my house and are still there today.

Although the lucid days were there, they became less frequent. I never knew what dad I was going to see when I walked in each day. Some days he was asleep and could not be woken. On other days he was hallucinating and talking to the television. Sometimes he would look at us in absolute terror as he talked about purple slime that was on him and would ask us to remove things from his body that weren't there. Then there were the days he was super loving and would say "I love you" hundreds of times in a row.

The hardest days to witness were those when he was in so much pain he would cry out to God. Although he was paralyzed, he apparently did have sensations in his arms, and they developed severe neuropathy. Over the years, he asked several family members and friends to help him commit suicide because the pain was so severe. We would medicate him as much as we could, but sometimes that wasn't enough.

I clearly remember one night when my sister, mom, and I were playing cards next to his bed. He kept asking us for help, and we had already given him all the medication we were allowed to give him. We kept telling him that we were so sorry he was hurting and that we loved him. It may sound callous to hear that we played cards as he yelled for help, but you have to understand, this went on for four and half years. We had to develop some of our own coping mechanisms, and sometimes blocking it out was all we could do. But that night, I remember him yelling, "God! Help me! Don't forget me! I'm still here! Help me." We all got tears in our eyes, stopped to love on him for a minute, then went back to cards. We were doing all we could do.

I must admit that I struggled with my faith in God during these years. I didn't understand (and still don't) why my dad was allowed to suffer so badly for so long. Nothing was terminal about his condition, so his situation was seemingly indefinite. We had no idea how long it would go on. We tried to go on with life as best we could. I worked and visited multiple times a week. We took him out to eat, to events, and even once took him on vacation. But I found myself angry with God and overwhelmed with the helplessness we all felt.

My dad passed away in March of 2012, and I was in the room with my mom when he took his last breath. It was a moment I will never forget. Throughout the week prior to his death, his body had begun shutting down. He was not conscious, and his body temperature slowly lowered as the days passed. We all gathered in his bedroom, went through boxes of pictures, laughed at old memories, and prepared for his funeral. We watched as his respirations slowed by the day and his time on this earth drew to an end.

My mom woke early that morning and came to get me out of bed, telling me that she thought it was time. As we watched, his breaths came the last couple of times and then finally stopped. At that moment, I felt the presence of God like I have never felt before or since. It was as if God was reaching a hand down from heaven, taking my dad by the hand, and saying, "Come on. Your suffering is over. You don't have to hurt anymore." Just like that, his spirit was gone. My mom and I both looked at each other, smiled, and said, "He is gone." My dad was no longer hurting. He was running and jumping in heaven with Jesus. He was free.

The strangest thing happened to all of us that day. My sisters, my mom, and I were all together, visiting the funeral home and preparing for his funeral. It feels funny to admit this, but we laughed all day! We went out to eat and giggled. We sat in the funeral home and giggled. It was such an odd thing that the director of the funeral home came in to see who was laughing in a funeral home. Yep, we laughed all day. My precious daddy wasn't hurting anymore, and we would get to see him someday. We had a lot of reasons to celebrate.

It is no surprise that during these four and half years I had several instances of heart palpitations and passed out at work a couple times. I tried to act like everything was fine and even convinced myself that I wasn't stressed out. I honestly believed it when I told people I didn't understand why I was passing out, because I was fine. "I'm used to what is happening with my dad. Really, I'm fine!" After several hospitalizations and tests on my heart, they told me it was stress. Go figure.

The next part of my story is the best part. It is the part where I make a decision to help myself and the part where I turn to God. It is the victory! You see, while I had been very lost and apart from God for so many years, God was waiting for me. He wasn't just waiting for me, he was pursuing me. And while I had spent years looking everywhere else for happiness, I had not looked toward my heavenly Father. The journey back to a relationship with God was going to be a difficult one, but God had never left me and wasn't about to give up on me.

Do You Believe?

All Scripture is God-breathed and is useful for teaching, rebuking, correcting and training in righteousness.

– 2 Timothy 3:16

Two years ago, I found myself emotionally and spiritually lost, and I felt powerless to do anything about it. As a wife, sister, daughter, and dog mom, I was overly dependent on my husband, overwhelmed with taking care of my house and property, and feeling scared all the time. I was overrun with thoughts of self-harm and engaging in quite a few self-destructive behaviors. I wasn't happy, and I didn't understand why.

When people asked me what was so wrong with my life to make me feel the way I did, I couldn't tell them. Nothing was bad at home, I liked my life, and I had a husband I loved being around who cherished me and made me laugh every day. I had a job I enjoyed, three precious dogs, a small supportive family, and a handful of good friends. I had a nice home, a nice car, a pool, and a beautiful yard (this has always been a passion of mine). I couldn't understand why I felt the way I did. I just knew that I was tired of it, and I had to do something.

What I want to share with you next are some of the things I did to help myself and how I did them. My hope is that something you read will help you find some strength, peace, and healing.

What Is Your Decision?

Let me begin this last and most important section of my book by asking you a few questions:

Do you believe that the Bible is the word of God?

Do you believe it is true?

Do you believe that God says what he means and means what he says?

Do you believe that what God says in the Bible applies to you?

These are some questions I want you to wrestle with before moving on in this book. Your answers will play a huge part in how much this last section will help you in your struggles. I mention in the introduction that much of what I have to say is not rocket science or super spiritual. I'm not a minister, and I am fairly new to studying the Bible. However, the Bible does play a crucial role in my healing, and in fact, I don't believe any of us can heal without it. The truth contained in the Bible has helped me to turn my life around. I believe that it can help you too. But you must believe that it is true. You have to believe that it applies to you and that God means what he says.

Up until the past year and a half, I didn't know how to read the Bible. What I mean is that of course I can read it, but there is so much to read I didn't know where to start. Some of it is tedious. Some of it seems irrelevant. Some of it is shocking, and some of it seems overused. I have heard the usual Bible stories: David and Goliath, Noah's ark, Zacchaeus in his tree, Jonah and the fish, Jesus healing people, and the crucifixion story. Yes, I believed that the Bible is true and that God is not a liar. I knew about heaven and hell, and I knew God has some things he doesn't want us to do. I knew that he is a good God who sent his Son to die for our sins and that he was raised from the dead, and so forth and so on, but I didn't see how any of this applied to my life.

I knew all this stuff about the Bible, but it didn't seem to be helping me. As a result of my resistant attitude, I never picked up my Bible and read it. I read the occasional quote in a social media meme or on the flip calendar on my desk at work, but before any healing could take place in my life, I had to figure out how to get God's truth into my heart. If I believed that everything in the Bible was true, then I needed to know what it said. I needed to think like it was true, feel like it was true, and act like it was true. I wasn't doing any of those things.

Even though I was lost and had so many misconceptions about God and myself, God never gave up on me. As you are about to read, he was calling me to himself. He was sending people into my life who would help me see his love and the hope that comes in believing in him. He was going to heal the fragile heart of a little girl who felt so unloved and unwanted. I may have been an adult, but the little girl inside me still felt tolerated, not wanted.

Putting it simply, if you don't believe that God is telling the truth, you are basically calling God a liar. That may sound harsh, but I don't know any other way to say it. And I would encourage you to reconsider your position. I cannot find anything bad that could come from believing God and believing in God. If you can relate to anything I have said about depression, anxiety, and self-defeating behaviors, what do you have to lose? If you want to improve your life and feel better, why not give God a try? What you are doing isn't working, so try something different!

If you choose to try things God's way, what have you lost? You behave as a kind, honest, decent human being. You get guidance on how to be the best person you can be. You find someone to lean on in times of trouble, and you get the most amazing reward when you pass away. But what if you are wrong? Well, not only do you miss out on all these blessings God offers, but there is this place called hell that I imagine you want no part of.

So, give God a try. I promise he has nothing but good things to say about you and your future. The Bible says that nothing can separate us from the love of God. Thank goodness!

For I am convinced that neither death nor life, neither angels nor demons, neither the present nor the future, nor any powers, neither height nor depth, nor anything else in all creation, will be able to separate us from the love of God that is in Christ Jesus our Lord.

– Romans 8:38–39

The LORD your God is with you,
 the Mighty Warrior who saves.
He will take great delight in you;
 in his love he will no longer rebuke you,
 but rejoice over you with singing.

– Zephaniah 3:17

"For I know the plans I have for you," declares the LORD, "plans to prosper you and not to harm you, plans to give you a hope and a future."

– Jeremiah 29:11

But you, Lord, are a compassionate and gracious God, slow to anger, abounding in love and faithfulness.

– Psalm 86:15

Now, back to my question. If you believe the Bible is the word of God and God means what he says, I have a couple more questions I want to ask you:

Do you want to get better?

Do you want to help yourself?

What are you willing to do to help yourself?

Now you have another decision to make: the decision to help yourself.

I found myself lying in bed or on the couch feeling so hopeless and defeated. I did occasionally ask God to help me or pray for his strength. But truth be told, I wanted God to do all the work. I wanted him to make all the negative thoughts go away and heal me. I wanted him to fix my life while I stayed at home in my safe zone. I didn't want to do anything. I lacked the desire to attend church or deal with uncomfortable things from my past. I wanted a cure without having to go to the doctor and take my medicine.

Getting to Church

The Lord is my rock, my fortress and my deliverer; my God is my rock, in whom I take refuge.

– Psalm 18:2

Then we will no longer be infants, tossed back and forth by the waves, and blown here and there by every wind of teaching and by the cunning and craftiness of people in their deceitful scheming. Instead, speaking the truth in love, we will grow to become in every respect the mature body of him who is the head, that is, Christ. From him the whole body, joined and held together by every supporting ligament, grows and builds itself up in love, as each part does its work.

– Ephesians 4:14–16

I have spent almost thirty years away from the Methodist church of my childhood. Early in our marriage, Greg explained to me that, although he would follow me to church, he probably wouldn't lead me there. He knew that the Bible gave him the role of the spiritual leader of our home, and he admitted that he was not fulfilling his duty. But he had his own struggles, and I had to focus on helping myself. I couldn't afford to waste any more time waiting for him to get on board. If I was going to get to church, I had to find my own way. And I had so many excuses that kept me away for so long:

- I'm too tired
- It is too cold, and my husband will have to wear a hat, and people will stare
- I can't dress up because dresses and Crocs look stupid together

- Sunday is my only day to relax since I clean on Saturdays
- I need to sleep in
- I didn't belong there
- I can't go by myself
- It's raining

The list could go on and on, but they were all excuses that the enemy had planted in my mind. You see, Satan did not want me in church. He didn't want me to learn the truth about who he is, and he sure didn't want me to know the truth about who God is. Satan wanted me to stay defeated and to fail at any attempts I made to fight back. And whatever attempts I did make to fight back, he wanted me to do it alone.

For years, I convinced myself that I didn't have to go to church. I told myself that if I believed in the crucifixion story, asked Jesus into my heart, and occasionally prayed, that was enough. I have talked with believers who do not think they need "organized religion." They argue that a personal relationship with God can be accomplished without church. And while attending church isn't required to have a personal relationship with God, I do believe that it is *vital* to our success as Christians. As I will talk about in the next chapter, we are in a battle that we are not meant to fight alone. I know that for me, trying to fight it on my own wasn't working.

God designed us to be relational creatures. He designed us to help each other and support each other. From what I can tell, even all the way back in the Old Testament, people gathered together to worship and learn about God. They prayed to God and cried out to God. Sometimes they did it alone, but more often they did it together. Jesus and his disciples were together almost constantly. Jesus taught them about God, they talked about God to anyone who would listen, and they spent time together praising God. Then Jesus sent the disciples out to teach others about God. It was at this point that churches were born.

In Matthew 16:18, Jesus tells Peter (whose name means "rock") that he will be the foundation of the church. The *church* is the place where believers can go to find solid ground to stand on. Church is where people learn about God, praise God, hold each other accountable, and support each other. It is not a building but a group of people. It is a group of people who gather to offer the truth about salvation and study about how God wants us to live. It is a place where God uses relationships among believers to bring us closer to him.

> And let us consider how we may spur one another on toward love and good deeds, not giving up meeting together, as some are in a habit of doing, but encouraging one another.
>
> – Hebrews 10:24–25

My first step toward getting myself back on track was to get back to church. And it was *hard*. I had been away from church for so long. I knew it was something I needed to do, but I couldn't seem to make it happen. Nothing at all against the church where I was raised, but I didn't want to go back there. So many people knew me, and I felt judged (one of Satan's tactics). I wanted to go to a church where I could get a fresh start. I was hoping for a place where no one knew my background and my family. What I found was a place where I was seen, loved, and supported.

After talking about it with friends for several months, I heard good things about a church near my house. A friend said it was very casual and had a reputation for loving God and people. I could wear jeans and Crocs, which made me very happy. I talked to Greg about it for a few weeks, and he agreed to give it a try. For me, the fact that it was not a huge church was both a good thing and a God thing. I think I would have been lost in a big church and have had trouble getting involved.

If you are like me and have trouble going into social situations alone, I encourage you to make a plan. I would suggest that you begin by asking around. Ask your friends about their churches. Do some research. Go with someone you know to their church. Getting there the first time is often the hardest part. I am not sure I would have ever made it there without Greg by my side.

After a few months of persistent discussion, Greg and I finally managed to get there. This in itself was a miracle because Greg had as many excuses as I did. Between the two of us, the odds of us ever making it there were not very high. But I wanted to get better, and somewhere deep down I knew that the answers were at church—not the building but in the teaching and the worship and the fellowship. After all, what I had been doing only seemed to be taking me further and further away from God's promise of peace and joy. The only place I could go was up.

We found a Sunday that was perfect weather when neither of us was too tired. I knew that if Greg was there, his outgoing personality would make it easy for me. I have always been OK if he was there. He never meets a stranger, and as usual, he carried the conversations that day. He made a positive impression on everyone we met, as I quietly stood to the side and took it all in. I wasn't sure that anyone even noticed I was there (lies from Satan again), which is a typical feeling around Greg. But at least he helped get me there. That was half the battle.

But this day, because I was obedient in showing up, God met me there. The people were very friendly, the worship was genuine, and the sermon was powerful. The sermon series they were beginning was called, "I Am Not a Quitter." That was certainly fitting for the battle I was about to fight.

As soon as the service was over, I heard a voice yell, "Kathy! Kathy!" I looked up to see my cousin waving her arms in the air with a big smile on her face. I can hardly describe the relief I felt when I realized that I knew someone there. We hadn't seen each other in years and had never been close. But she knew me and my skin issues. And the hug I got from her that day let me know that she loved me. I didn't know at the time how much she loved Jesus, but God did. And he made sure that we connected that day!

Over the next few weeks, I continued to go despite Greg staying home most of the time. His body was failing, and his low energy level outweighed his desire to attend. If I was to keep attending church, I'd have to go by myself. And God knew that going by myself would be a huge task for me, so he made sure that my cousin saw me that day. If she had not seen me, I probably wouldn't have gone back.

Over the next few months, I continued to attend on Sundays and made it a priority to save my Saturday nights for rest. If I was going to get up early on a Sunday, I had to be in bed at a decent hour. Although it was difficult, I had a person to sit with at church and someone to greet me with a familiar hug. I had my comfy clothes and was delighted to learn that they would let me bring my Diet Dr. Pepper. They even had snacks and hot chocolate! (It's the little things, right?) I was immediately welcomed by some of my cousin's friends, and we all staked claim to the back row. I felt safe and welcomed.

The problem was, just showing up on Sundays wasn't enough. I had to find a way to get involved. Fortunately, this church believed in the importance of small group Bible studies. I was quickly recruited by my cousin to attend one that met on Sunday mornings. The same old excuses were there: *I don't have time. I don't want to get up that early on the weekend.* But, friends, you cannot fight the battle you are fighting by yourself. That is why God calls us to go to church. And he calls us not only to show up but to get involved.

The Enemy

> *The great dragon was hurled down— that ancient serpent called the devil, or Satan, who leads the whole world astray. He was hurled to the earth, and his angels with him.*
>
> *– Revelation 12:9*

You have heard me refer to Satan a few times in this book. Perhaps, like me, you don't really understand who the enemy is and how he works. I knew from the book of Genesis how Satan took the form of a snake in the garden of Eden and convinced Adam and Eve they didn't need to do things God's way. I knew that Satan tempted Jesus on several occasions. I even knew that Satan wanted to tempt me to sin and to keep me from accepting who God says I am. And I have heard some of the Scriptures about Satan, but I never took them to heart.

And while I don't want to spend a lot of time talking about him, I do think it is critical that we know who he is and how he operates. Rest assured, I am going to tell you how to defeat him, but indulge me as I give you a little bit of information about our enemy.

Let me begin with the following Scripture:

> For our struggle is not against flesh and blood, but against the rulers, against the authorities, against the powers of this dark world and against the spiritual forces of evil in the heavenly realms.
>
> – Ephesians 6:12

Now, if you believe that what the Bible says is true, then you can see here that the enemy is not a person. The enemy is not your past, nor is it your circumstances, your thoughts, or your feelings. The enemy is Satan. And the way I see it, he has help. The words *rulers*, *authorities*, *powers*, and *forces* are all plural. So, it isn't just Satan; he has helpers.

Let me show you a few verses about how the Bible describes Satan. I've italicized some words for emphasis.

> You belong to your father, the devil, and you want to carry out your father's desires. He was a *murderer* from the beginning, not holding to the truth, for there is no truth in him. When he lies, he speaks his native language, for he is a liar and the *father of lies*.
>
> – John 8: 44 (NIV)

> The thief comes only to *steal and kill and destroy*.
>
> – John 10:10 (NIV)

> Be alert and of sober mind. Your enemy the devil prowls around like a roaring *lion* looking for someone to *devour*.
>
> – 1 Peter 5:8 (NIV)

Did you catch all that? Our enemy is a murderer, a liar, and a thief who wants to devour and destroy us. Satan wants to destroy you. He is cunning and manipulative. He is good at what he does (but not good enough—more on that soon). Satan's goal is to keep us as far away from God as possible. He wants us defeated, afraid, and sad. He wants to destroy our relationships, our testimony, our livelihood, and our lives. He uses lies to convince us that we are unforgivable and unlovable. Satan's lies are so crafty that we don't even realize he is lying to us.

The lies that Satan uses against us are too many to name. I think Satan knows each of us very well and understands how to attack us where we are the weakest. He used my life with ichthyosis and my mistakes against me on a regular basis. The lies he tells me may be different from the lies he tells you. Here are a few examples of those he told me:

- You are unforgivable.
- God doesn't want you.
- God doesn't love you.
- You are a horrible person.
- You are defective.
- People don't like you.
- People are repulsed by you.
- You are ugly.
- You don't deserve to exist.
- There is no hope of you ever getting better.

Everything Satan tries to tell us is lies. But how do we recognize the lies? We must compare it to what God says about us in the Bible. We have to look at God's truth and know God's truth. We need to get it into our souls, and I'm going to show you how.

While I had found my way back to church, I didn't yet grasp that the battle I was fighting was going to get even more intense. Satan, that lion seeking to devour me, was not happy! He threw every lie he could think of at me. Although I was at church on Sundays, my thoughts during the week were still very dark and self-accusing. I felt even more unforgivable and unlovable than I did before I started going to church again.

I kept thinking, *God? How is this possible? I am going to church. I am taking this step. Why are things so much harder than before? I would be better off staying home.* Again, this was Satan. The more steps I took toward pursuing the truth, the more lies he threw my way. I even remember a couple of times, as I sat on the back row, that I almost audibly heard, "You don't deserve to be here. You are a murderer!"

Satan is such a punk.

My problem, and maybe yours, was that I didn't know what God said about me. And not only was I *not* trying to find out, but I didn't even know where to start.

Steps to Victory

For the word of God is alive and active. Sharper than any double-edged sword, it penetrates even to dividing soul and spirit, joints and marrow; it judges the thoughts and attitudes of the heart.

– Hebrews 4:12

About the same time that I began going to church again, a friend asked me if I wanted to join her on a journey to read the Bible in one year through a cell phone app. She said it would take only twenty minutes a day and would include a part of the Old and New Testament as well as a Psalm or Proverb. I agreed to participate because—let me say it again—I wanted to get better. I knew it would take time out of my day, but it was better to lie in bed and read God's Word than to lie in bed and worry.

What I liked about the app is that it reintroduced me to the books of the Bible and the stories I had long forgotten. It also had an audio function so I could listen to the Scripture, which can really help those of us who are auditory learners. Each day was paired with a devotional to start off the reading, and I was given an opportunity to ask questions at the end, which I did often.

My favorite part about this app was the videos. There were eight- to twelve-minute videos that gave the overview of each book of the Bible. It was beneficial for me to see the forest instead of the trees—that is, the overall story. It helped me link together the storyline and what the author of each book was teaching me about God. One thing I noticed was how time and time again the people in the Bible failed God. They messed up big time—over and over. God would get angry with them, but he would eventually forgive them and use them to further his kingdom. If God could use these sinful, messed up people to bring glory to his name, maybe he could do something with the mess I called my life.

For me, the women's small group at my church was where the rubber met the road. That is where I learned to really dig in and get to know God. I cannot emphasize enough the importance this played in my healing. Up to this point, every time I tried to read the Bible I didn't know where to start, and I didn't understand half of what I read. I would have trouble focusing and feel frustrated with my confusion. I have since learned that this was the enemy trying to keep me stuck and hopeless. But as soon as I got into a Bible study, that changed for me. Suddenly, I had a guide. I had a starting point, commentary about what I was reading with questions to answer. I loved curling up on my bed, listening to my dogs snoring, and answering the questions in the workbook.

I know what you are thinking: *You actually like doing a workbook?* Yes, I was the kid who loved to do schoolwork growing up. Homework wouldn't put me down or say something ugly to me. In fact, it made me feel good to get it done. There was a sense of victory when it was completed, and the same seemed to happen when I did my workbooks about God. These workbooks required me to look up specific Scriptures for myself—Scriptures that helped me and which the books did not write out for me. Instead, they told me where to go, and I had to do the work. Although it seems counterintuitive, having to look them up myself helped.

The thought of doing Bible studies and workbooks may seem too cumbersome for you. Maybe you think you don't have time, or you don't like to write. But hear me when I say that studying the Bible in this way got me face-to-face with God's truth. It allowed me to begin getting to know what God says about me. It allowed me to get familiar with God's character, understand what the Bible was saying, and ask all the questions I wanted.

Some weeks I didn't feel like I had the time to do the study, but it was so beneficial I made the time. What's more, getting the chance to talk about what I was learning with my small group was priceless. I'm not saying it was always easy. The enemy did not want me in that Bible study, and, as much as he could, he tried to keep me from going or from sharing once I got there. He often attempted to keep me from attending church afterward. Occasionally, walking from one part of the building to the sanctuary after our small group seemed impossible. I had to fight the urge to run out the door. But I was learning and growing closer to God, and growing often involves pain.

It is not by accident that my first Bible study ever was about how to fight the enemy. It was called *The Armor of God* by Priscilla Shirer. I highly recommend it because it was during this study that some truths really hit home for me. The most important truth was that I am in a battle. The final battle was won when Jesus died and rose again. But the daily battles I experience while on earth are ones that I can't win alone. Priscilla's book is based on Ephesians 6:10–17:

> Finally, be strong in the Lord and in his mighty power. Put on the full armor of God, so that you can take your stand against the devil's schemes. For our struggle is not against flesh and blood, but against the rulers, against the authorities, against the powers of this dark world and against the spiritual forces of evil in the heavenly realms. Therefore put on the full armor of God, so that when the day of evil comes, you may be able to stand your ground, and after you have done everything, to stand. Stand firm then, with the belt of truth buckled around your waist, with the breastplate of righteousness in place, and with your feet fitted with the readiness that comes from the gospel of peace. In addition to all this, take up the shield of faith, with which you can extinguish all the flaming arrows of the evil one.

Take the helmet of salvation and the sword of the Spirit, which is the word of God.

I learned that Satan is relentless and cunning. He has been attacking me and lying to me for years. He has convinced me of so many of his lies that I had given up and given in. He had deceived me for so long that I stopped fighting. I believed that I was unforgivable, unlovable, and unwanted.

As I began to look at my life as a war, I made a decision. Satan may have won many battles, but he wasn't going to win the war. This meant that I had to get ready to fight! I had to stop waiting for God to do it all and prepare myself for battle. I wanted to get better, and I was willing to fight back.

In her book, Priscilla Shirer does an excellent job of explaining each piece of the armor that God has given us. She describes what each piece looks like and how we can get suited up to fight. One of my favorite parts of her study is when she talks about the shields that were used by the Roman soldiers. She describes how sometimes the enemy would send fireballs out of the sky during battle. To protect themselves from the fireballs, the soldiers would work together. They would come together in a circle and put their shields together over their head. She described this as the turtle formation. This made a lot of sense to me and helped me understand why I needed my small group.

The point is we cannot fight this battle alone. We need each other. We need other Christians around us who can pray with us and for us. We need other Christians who we can call on when fireballs are falling in our lives.

Again, I urge you to go to church and get involved in a small group. We are not going to win this battle alone. In fact, God *designed* us to fight together. My small group and I have a group text in which any of us can ask for prayer at any time. What a wonderful feeling to know that they are there, ready to huddle around me when I need it.

Resisting the Enemy

Your word is a lamp for my feet, a light on my path.

– Psalm 119:105

Through continued attendance at my small group and completion of my weekly Bible studies, I began to get familiar with some Scriptures about who God is and who I am to God. I had spent forty-eight years believing that I was unforgivable, unlovable, defective, gross—you remember the list. I was being deceived by an enemy that wanted to destroy me. It was necessary to begin the process of getting to know what God says about each of these beliefs because God's opinion of me is the only one that matters. And since I believe what God says is true, I had to make a choice to change my thinking and begin acting like it is true. I had to get God's truths imprinted on my heart instead of buying all the junk Satan had been selling me.

It was through my Bible studies that I learned more about Satan. First, he is not omniscient. I have read a great deal about this fact, and it appears to be indisputable among biblical experts. The word *omniscient* means "all knowing" and does not apply to Satan. He doesn't know what we are going to do, what our future holds, and or what we are thinking. Nothing in the Bible suggests he can read our minds. One of his tactics is to throw negative thoughts and temptations our way, hoping something will stick. He accuses us, reminds us of our mistakes, and condemns us. He tempts us to sin by making it look so good. Then he points a shaming finger at us the minute we take the bait. He has done it to me, and he does it to you. His tactics never change.

Satan tried to convince me that I am the worst person in the world because of my sin. I believed there was no way God would ever want me. Boy, was I wrong! The truth is that Jesus died so that we don't have to pay for our sins. Are we guilty? Yes. None of us are righteous. But because Jesus was willing to take our punishment, God has wiped away all the charges against us. I learned that I don't have to punish myself anymore because Jesus took my punishment for me.

> For all have sinned and fall short of the glory of God, and all are justified freely by his grace through the redemption that came by Christ Jesus.
>
> – Romans 3:23–24

I never understood what *justified* means, and perhaps you don't either. I now understand it to mean that God has declared us "not guilty." God isn't a liar either. He means what he says, so we need to act like it is true. To refuse his forgiveness and Jesus's sacrifice would be the ultimate disrespect to God. It would be like someone giving you the grandest, most expensive gift in the world. You open the gift, look at it, and decide that you don't deserve it, so you give it back. That is what we are doing when we refuse to accept forgiveness. I imagine that God is very offended when we tell him that we don't want this amazing gift.

I also learned that Satan must yield to God. He is powerful but not as powerful as our God. Satan cannot destroy us, but he can make us miserable. He can make futile our efforts to live as God created us. But hear me when I say that Satan may be powerful, but our God is *all* powerful. God has actually already defeated him. The Bible says that we, as children of God, are seated with Jesus in heaven next to God (Ephesians 2:6). We are his children, and our inheritance is waiting for us in heaven.

I have often wondered if God has already won the battle, then why am I getting beat up? What I didn't realize is that our reward, our inheritance as children of God, won't be given to us until we get to heaven. So, in the meantime we live in a broken world where Satan and his buddies run wild. While we are on earth, Satan is going to try to get to us any way he can. But here is the cool part.

Satan *must* flee when we use our authority as children of God. We don't have to give him the time of day. We can just send him packing. James 4:7 says, "Resist the devil, and he will flee from you." We must say it out loud since there is nothing in the Bible that says Satan can read our minds. This was an important revelation for me because I had never told Satan out loud to leave me alone. In fact, I have sat in church and allowed him to tell me that I didn't deserve to be there, that what I did to my baby was unforgivable, and that God didn't want me. He had me convinced that Jesus's blood covered everyone else's sin except mine. Learning the importance of telling Satan to go away was an important revelation for me, because once I do so, he must flee. He has no choice—and he knows it.

On my worst nights, I found myself so overwhelmed with darkness that I was unable to speak out loud. It sounds silly, but I have since read of other people having the same experience. It felt like something had me by the throat and I could not make a sound. I thought I was going crazy. But I now realize our enemy is resourceful. He knows that he doesn't have to leave until I tell him to, so he tried to keep me from speaking.

I spent years struggling at night, letting Satan beat me up. I spent hours feeling overwhelmed with shame and condemnation. I would lie in my bed, hating myself, afraid that I would never get better. And Satan wanted to keep it that way. I would occasionally be able to pray in those moments, but my thoughts would race so fast that even that was hard. Prayer is one thing that Satan cannot stop us from doing, but he does try to find ways to make it difficult.

Sometimes Christian music helped calm my thoughts. I am a huge fan of Christian music and believe that God uses it to seek our praise and encourage us. Sometimes I would reach out to a friend via text and tell them what was happening. The friend would coach me to tell Satan to leave me alone. "I can't!" was all I could say in reply. I had to get a better plan. I had to be smarter than my enemy.

My Battle Plan

My battle plan included something I discovered in Neil Anderson's book, *The Bondage Breaker*. In this book, Neil gives a list of truths about who we are in Christ and Scripture to support each truth. I recorded myself reading each truth and Scripture into my phone. On those nights when I was unable to speak, I would play that recording. I would play it over and over until I could read them out loud in the moment. It was amazing how well it worked. It upsets me that I hadn't previously known about this whole "command Satan and he must go" thing—well, I believe I had heard it before but just didn't take it literally.

Satan is the father of lies, and it was going to take some strategic planning on my part to be ready for him. I found Neil Anderson's list extremely helpful. The list included statements such as *I am a child of God, I am forgiven, I have been justified, I am loved.* Each statement was followed by the supporting verse from the Bible. I made copies of these verses and kept them with me. I had copies in my backpack, my bedroom, and my office at work. I could pull them out and read them at any time. I even took pictures of the pages in his book and kept them on my phone. Remember, if I believed what God says, then I had to make a choice to learn it and make it part of who I am.

With the encouragement of my small group, I picked two verses to memorize that would help me with my anxiety. I wrote the verses on note cards and posted them in several places in my home:

> For God has not given us a spirit of fear and timidity, but of power, love and of self-discipline.
>
> – 2 Timothy 1:7 (NLT)

> So do not fear, for I am with you; do not be dismayed, for I am your God. I will strengthen you and help you.
>
> – Isaiah 41:10

I would read these verses over and over, inserting my name into them: "Kathy, do not fear, for I am with you. Do not be dismayed, Kathy. I am your God. I will strengthen and help you." I was beginning to see that my self-defeating thoughts were Satan's way of trying to take me out, and I was not going to believe him anymore. It was a deliberate choice I had to make at times, and it wasn't always easy. Easy would have been to do nothing. Easy would have been *not* writing those Scriptures on those cards. Easy would have been *not* reading or memorizing them.

Let me say something about that word *easy*. As I was beginning to get familiar with God's Word, I kept looking for the verse that says if you believe in God and follow his commands, bad things won't happen, everything will be fine, you won't have to fight any more. Well, guess what? It isn't there. There is no Scripture that says the Christian life will be easy. In fact, the closer I get to God, the harder the enemy comes at me. The problem for him was that I was learning to arm myself for battle. I was finally in a church with a small group of soldiers surrounding me. I was learning how to fight. It was never easy, and I still don't do it perfectly. But God is bigger than anything the enemy brings at me.

I slowly began to do what the Bible tells us to do about taking every thought captive. In 2 Corinthians 10:3–5, Paul says, "For though we live in the world, we do not wage war as the world does. The weapons we fight with are not the weapons of the world. On the contrary, they have divine power to demolish strongholds. We demolish arguments and every pretension that sets itself up against the knowledge of God, and we take captive every thought to make it obedient to Christ." Since we have thoughts every waking minute of the day, this proved to be a difficult task for me. I spent years believing every thought that went through my head. I never stopped to ask whether those thoughts lined up with what God says about me. Satan attacks our mind the most, probably because our thoughts lead to our feelings, and our feelings lead to our actions. So if he can get us thinking down the wrong path, he can get us behaving down the wrong path.

The more I learned, the more proactive I became. The more proactive I became, the more I was able to win the daily battles. I used to spend days, weeks, and months thinking I was defective and unforgivable. I know it had to break God's heart to see me suffering needlessly. But soon I was learning and getting better at using the weapons I had at my disposal.

I wonder what my neighbors think when I am mowing grass and yell aloud, "Shut up, Satan! Leave me alone. God says that isn't true!" My mom has always told me never to say, "Shut up," but in this case, I think it is quite fitting. I have screamed it when working outside, and I have whispered it when arguing with my husband. I have learned that just because I *think* it does not make it true. A thought is just a thought. It can't hurt me, and I don't have to keep thinking about it. I don't always notice the lie right away, and every now and then I do fall back into old habits. But I win more battles than I lose, which is a big improvement.

Another thing I did to help myself was to write down some prayers and tape them to my wall. I took pictures of them and would read them on my phone before I walked into the building at work. I recorded myself reading them too. I'll share a few with you because I want you to understand how deliberate I had to be. I was taking this battle seriously.

God, I believe that everything you say about me is true. Help me to recognize destructive and unhealthy thoughts quickly, and help me to rehearse my true identity in you until it is part of my soul.

God, thank you for the gift of your Son and for forgiving me when I fail to be the person you want me to be. Thank you for all your gifts. Help me to unpack them and use them. Help me to recognize the real enemy, discern his attacks, and take action to thwart his plans.

God, I know that your way is the only way! I need to know what you say about me, my future, my beliefs, and my behavior. Lead me to the truth you want me to know, and imprint it on my heart.

God, you say that I am forgiven, and I believe you. You say that you love me and that you will never leave me. I believe you. Thank you for being there in the darkest times. Teach me to hold up my shield of faith and defeat feelings and thoughts of fear. Show me how to act according to your will.

My prayers were nothing fancy or complicated. I wrote them down so my enemy couldn't muddle my thoughts to keep me from praying. All I had to do was read them. I recorded them so that when I couldn't say them I could hear them. This is still something I have to do from time to time. And I have added to my prayers as well.

Sometimes I still spend hours or days spiraling into a dark tunnel before I realize where I am. At that point, finding the strength to climb out of the tunnel can be grueling. It is like pulling your shoe out of deep mud only to take another step and pull up the other shoe. So, I needed all the help I could get.

Before I move on, let me give you some words of encouragement. Be patient with yourself. It is a battle. Remember, there is no easy button. But so far, you have been losing the battle. Wouldn't you like to win? I do! Get up and get moving. Take small steps. Find a church and show up. Then find a small group and get involved in a Bible study. Seek out what God says about you. Find verses that relate to your own struggles. Memorize a few of them and put the rest in easy to find places. Write down a few prayers. Don't sit there and let the enemy beat you up. Fight back! Record yourself reading some Bible verses, and play them as often as you need to hear them. Choose to tell the enemy, "I am a child of God. I am loved by him and forgiven. You are a liar, and I command you to leave me alone."

Covering All the Bases

Although my relationship with God, beliefs about myself, and my spiritual strength were improving, something else was going on with me. I just couldn't seem to get myself completely unstuck. It felt as if I had one leg still trapped in quicksand. Greg and I discussed the possibility that I might need the help of a doctor and, possibly, even a counselor. I had come too far to give up now, so I kept moving forward.

Medication

It was not easy to tell my doctor the truth about how I was feeling and what I was thinking. But God blessed me with a doctor who listened with compassion and made some wise suggestions about medication. She taught me that there are "feel-good" chemicals in our brains called serotonin and dopamine. She said that stress can cause a shortage of these chemicals, and medication can help.

I began taking medication that targeted one of these chemicals. Although I was improving, I still felt like something wasn't right. I went back to her after a few months, and we added a medication that targeted a different chemical. It turns out that I needed two medications to get me to a point where I could begin to help myself. And there is nothing wrong with that.

My decision to begin medication preceded my return to church and probably helped give me the motivation to attend that first service. Depression has this ability to make you feel stuck. You feel miserable and don't enjoy doing anything that usually makes you happy. You have nothing to give anyone, much less the energy to help yourself. And sometimes medication is what you need to get those feel-good chemicals balanced again.

Some of you may believe that taking medication is a cop-out. Maybe you have never taken medication and don't want to put those chemicals in your body. I have even met people who told me I needed to *choose* to be happy. Oh, how I wish it was that simple! I was desperate for relief from my pain. I wanted to leave no stone unturned, to say that I had tried everything. What I was doing with church and God's truth was helping, but it wasn't enough. Choosing to be happy wasn't an option for me. I don't feel guilty for taking medication for my diabetes or my skin disease. Taking medication for depression is no different.

If you are struggling with depression and anxiety, I would encourage you to talk with your doctor. Keep going back if you don't feel any improvement within a few weeks. Sometimes trying a different medication or adding one, as I did, helps. You don't have to tell anyone that you are on medication; it is none of their business. But you deserve to feel better. I felt as if I had a dark cloud around me all the time. Everything was difficult. Yes, Satan played a part in my struggles, but for me, medication needed to be part of the solution. It gave me the motivation and energy to begin fighting my way back.

Early in our marriage, my husband was struggling with depression. He had apparently been struggling with it long before we met. I convinced him to talk with his doctor, and she prescribed him an antidepressant. In a few weeks, he made a comment to me that I will never forget. He said, "For the first time in my life, I look forward to tomorrow." I was stunned! He was in his early forties and had suffered for so long. No one should have to live like that. God did not create you to feel miserable and hopeless. He created you to experience love and peace and joy.

Counseling

From the ends of the earth I call to you, I call as my heart grows faint; lead me to the rock that is higher than I.

– Psalm 61:2

The LORD is close to the brokenhearted and saves those who are crushed in spirit.

– Psalm 34:18

He heals the brokenhearted and binds up their wounds.

– Psalm 147: 3

I have saved this section for last because it is the part that I am afraid will scare many of you off. Just like social stigmas exist against taking medication, there's a black mark against seeking counseling. If you need counseling, you must be crazy or weak, right? No, not at all. Going to counseling means that you want to get better and you are willing to do the work. I had begun to see some relief from medication, but it was clear that I had some other things going on. It turns out that the origin of many of my problems came from trauma.

Asking for Help

I made one more difficult choice. I called my health insurance company and got a list of agencies where I could go to seek counseling. I searched several websites and was drawn to a certain one that was close to my home. I scanned through the list of counselors, their biographies, and their list of specialties. I ran across a picture of this blond woman, younger than me, with a light in her eyes. I swear it looked as if she was shining off the page at me.

Her list of specialties included treating depression, anger, self-harming behaviors, anxiety, ADHD, trauma, abuse, PTSD, and others. So I made the call. It was one of the most difficult but beneficial things I have done. Isn't it crazy how making a phone call can be so difficult? It was almost as tough as walking into church alone. But God had big things in store for me, and he gave me the strength to get it done.

On the day of my first appointment, I walked into the waiting room, and others were there waiting to see their counselor. I wondered what they were there to talk about and if they were crazy or if they thought I was crazy. I thought to myself, *If this doesn't work, I don't know what I'm going to do.* Then I did what I always do; I pretended that everyone else in the room was invisible and I was deaf. I stared at the floor, fought back the urge to run out of the room, and waited. When she came out and called my name, the kindness in her smile communicated that God had something special planned for me.

Although I didn't know it at the time, counseling turned out to be one of the ways God would bring tremendous healing to my life. I knew it wasn't going to work if I didn't want help and if I wasn't willing to talk. I would have to trust her. I'd have to talk about things that hurt and reveal things to her I had never told anyone else. I had to be willing to work at healing and cry in front of her—a lot—and step out of my comfort zone. I knew I would get frustrated with her and wasn't going to like everything she said, but that would have to be OK.

Although I liked her right away, it took several months for us to develop a trusting relationship. The relationship between counselor and client is probably the most critical part of the process. If you seek counseling and you find yourself unable to create a trusting relationship, find another counselor. But give it time first. It won't happen overnight. One of the mistakes many people make in going to counseling is that they rush the process. They want an immediate fix, and they want it to be easy. But it had taken me forty-eight years to get where I was, and it wasn't going to change overnight.

The first thing she and I did was take a look at my physical health and my medications. We went over all my medications, and I admitted to her that I wasn't taking some of them as they were prescribed. Sometimes I didn't take them at all, and other times I took too much. She told me I was being selfish, which shocked me. She explained that if I wanted to get better, I had to stop messing around and do what I knew I was supposed to do. Ouch! But she was right.

She suggested that I make myself signs that said, "TAKE YOUR MEDICINE" and hang them around my house. I made the signs, and they are still posted around my house today. Sometimes I still forget, which makes me human. But I take ownership of my mistakes and vow to do better.

Who Is on the Throne?

One of my earliest conversations with my counselor was about my husband and how he was my rock and my best friend. I told her that I felt safe around him and couldn't imagine being alive without him. I conveyed to her how close we are and that I don't like going on the "girl trips" my friends go on because I don't want to go anywhere without him. I told her that we even argue about which of us is going to die first and so we've decided we want to die at the same time. I remember telling her that I don't think I could breathe without him.

Her first real therapeutic comment to me was "Oh! That is all kinds of messed up!" My immediate reaction was to get defensive. "What's so wrong with being close to my husband? We are each other's hero. We don't want to live without each other." I'll divulge to you that this was not the only time I got angry with her. But her job was to help me, even if that meant telling me something I didn't want to hear. And if I wanted help, I had to think about what she said.

It took me a few months before I finally realized that I had put my husband on the throne. I had put all my faith, strength, and energy into another human being. Not only is that not what God wants for me, it isn't fair to my husband either. Making him the center of my world puts a great deal of pressure on him to be my everything. He is human, and he can't be my everything. Greg loves me dearly, but his love for me is nothing compared to the love God has for me. People will let us down. People will leave us. People will make mistakes. God will not do any of those things.

God is a jealous God, and he wants to be the *only* God in our life. To make him the center of my life, I had to learn about God and spend time with him. I had to turn to God first. I had to talk to God first. I had to make him my everything. Taking Greg off the throne is something I still struggle with, especially because of my skin issues. I have trouble believing that one man could ever love me, much less that I might find another when Greg is gone. After all, he is eighteen years older than me. But that part of life is inevitable. We lose people, but we never lose God. If I couldn't figure out how to make God the center of my world, I was going to have some seriously hard times. I had a lot of work to do.

Although I did not know it initially, my counselor is a Christian. I say that in the present tense because I still see her regularly. She loves God and knows quite a bit about the Bible. She brings Jesus and God's truth into every session, which is something I clearly need. I believe that for the believer this is an important criterion in choosing a counselor.

My counselor will say, "But what does God say about you, Kathy?" When I shrug my shoulders, she will tell me a Scripture describing how precious I am to God. And to be honest, I blew her off for a long while. The way I looked at it, she didn't know me yet! She didn't know the things I have done and how horrible I am. I believed that God may have allowed his only Son to die on the cross for others but—nope—not for me! God may forgive others but not me. God may love others but not me. I was someone who was tolerated, not wanted.

But she continued to remind me of some basic truths:

I am a child of God.

I am loved by God.

Jesus paid the price for my sin.

I am forgiven!

As it turns out, church and Bible study and medication and note cards and recordings of Scripture were not enough. There was something deep down, something that had been there most of my life, that was holding me down. I could tell myself all day long how God sees me, but it wasn't changing how I saw myself.

Trauma Processing

When my counselor told me she was trained in trauma processing, I explained to her that I haven't experienced any trauma. I haven't been in the military, I haven't witnessed a violent crime, and I haven't been abused. She chuckled and explained that trauma was an event or series of events that were deeply distressing or disturbing—like having a skin disease that affected every area of my life. Or having an abortion. OK, so maybe I had experienced some trauma (insert wide-eyed emoji here).

Trauma processing was by far the hardest part of my counseling experience. But God used it to reach me in a way I did not think possible. I want to take a little time to help you understand, in layman's terms, what trauma processing can entail.

As you may have seen on the news, trauma affects the brain. There are lots of people talking about trauma on social media, especially as it relates to educating children who have experienced trauma. I am sure you have heard about PTSD in soldiers who have gone to war. You probably know that they experience anxiety, depression, difficulty sleeping, flashbacks, nightmares, and more. Years ago, the mental health world believed that the best way to get past a traumatic event was to retell it over and over until it didn't hurt anymore. The problem was it didn't work.

The goal of trauma processing is to rewire the brain and change the beliefs related to the trauma. She used the analogy that the trauma I had experienced was like a big piece of glass that had been shattered, and those shattered pieces affected parts of my brain. To me, that glass represented my beliefs about myself. By processing the trauma, we could sweep up those broken shards of glass. Only then could I view the things that happened to me with more truth and clarity.

I needed to be able to see myself the way God saw me and separate myself from my skin. I have a couple of examples I would like to share with you because they were so incredibly powerful. My description is going to be a little oversimplified because I struggle to put it into words.

Part of trauma processing is something called tapping. Tapping involves me tapping my knees with an open palm, alternating left and right. She kept the rhythm, and I matched what she was doing. What this did was allow me to think about the trauma while also reminding a part of my brain that I am not there, I am here. It is similar to grounding, which involves various techniques to keep the body and brain connected to the present world. One example of grounding is having someone name five things they can see, four things they can hear, and three things they can feel touching their body. They may feel like a balloon floating off into space, but doing these quick exercises brings them back down to earth.

With trauma processing, the idea is that you talk about something painful from the past. As you talk, you allow yourself to experience the feelings and sensations that go along with that memory. As you permit the experience to run its course in your mind, you are tapping in the present. Tapping also does something called bilateral stimulation, which means that it activates both halves of the brain. The tapping not only served to keep me in the present, but it also activated both sides of my brain and allowed my brain to begin sweeping up the broken glass.

Changing My Views about Me

The first processing we did was related to my skin disease and how I saw myself. We focused initially on my earliest memory of the first day of first grade and the incident with the little boy who was having a meltdown because he was in my class. My belief about myself related to this incident was that I was unlovable and repulsive. I was someone that others wanted to get away from.

We went back through this scene several times, each time ending in tapping. I would then answer some questions about what I was feeling in my body. She would ask me how strongly I believed that I was unlovable. Through the process, the goal we set was to change this belief to *I am lovable*. It seems like a simple goal, but it was easier said than done. We would go back through the same memory again and again. More tapping. More questions. There were no right or wrong answers to her questions. I wasn't supposed to judge what was happening, just let it happen.

At one point she asked me to imagine that forty-eight-year-old Kathy walked into that classroom. What would she say to six-year-old Kathy? What would she do? I fought back tears as I played this through in my mind. More tapping and questions. Then we did the same thing again, only this time she asked me to imagine that Jesus walked into that classroom. What would he say? What would he do?

Tears began to fall down my cheeks as I saw him wrap me in his arms. Jesus told me that I was safe and loved and that he would never leave me. Same tapping. Same questions. How true do you believe it is that you are lovable? My answer to that question was beginning to change. But it was something we were going to have to revisit a few more times.

She explained to me that my brain would be a little foggy over the next few days because it was taking this new experience with Jesus and making it a part of how I think and feel. Going to work was difficult the next several days because I felt like I was looking at the world through glass. I had trouble focusing and completing tasks. The fog eventually lifted and, without even realizing it, this belief that I am lovable became something I could begin to believe. I *knew* that God loved me. I *knew* that he would never leave me.

We are still working on putting together my shattered view of myself. I know that God loves me, but I struggle with thoughts of feeling unwanted. At times, I still feel tolerated but never wanted by others. I don't mean that I feel this way toward my family because I know they love me and want me around. But outside my family and a couple of close friends, I struggle with feeling like anyone wants to be near me. And while this may not actually be true, it is how I feel periodically.

But because of my experience with trauma processing, things have gotten so much better. The enemy still tries to drag me down with thoughts like, "Nobody likes you," and "You aren't part of the cool crowd." Like I said before, I sometimes feel like everyone would be better off if I didn't exist. But I know this is a lie from Satan and try to work quickly to shut him up. The truth is that others may not want to be around me because of my skin, but that doesn't mean I don't deserve to be here and that God doesn't have a purpose for me. Sometimes I have to remind myself of this daily.

Accepting Forgiveness

The second processing I did was related to the abortion. My belief about that incident was that I was a horrible, unforgivable murderer. As I went back to the sights, sounds, and feelings of that experience, I had trouble staying in the present. I had put so much energy into pushing it out of my mind when it happened: *Don't feel it. Pretend it isn't happening.* When we processed it, I got so caught up in reliving it that we had to stop several times.

She would tell me to open my eyes. I could hear her, but I couldn't seem to make them open. "Tell me five things you can see," she would say, or "Four things you can hear." She would ask, "What color are your shoes?" She strived to keep me both in the present and in contact with those memories.

She asked me what I wanted to believe about the abortion. I told her I wanted to believe that what I did was OK. "Do you really think you will ever truly believe that it was OK?" she asked. No, I would never believe that what I did was OK. I had spent years and years unconsciously punishing myself for that one decision—a decision that God most certainly would not have supported. I decided my belief needed to be "Although I was wrong, I am forgiven."

Processing this event was tough. I tried to hide in my hoodie and behind my sunglasses. She made me take them off because she had to see my eyes. My legs bounced around as I resisted running out of the room. My hands got sweaty and my heart raced.

I made the mistake of going to work after our session. Bad idea! I was able to get through a couple of classes before I collapsed with the grief I had never let myself feel. I sat in the nurse's office, sobbing in the arms of a friend. She prayed for me and held me as I cried. I don't mean that I cried for a few minutes or only a few tears. I cried for a long time. I cried tears that I had spent twenty-one years holding back.

I was eventually able to calm down and drive myself home in a daze. I ended up having to apologize to my boss for my unprofessional behavior. I was embarrassed that I had lost control at work, and I wouldn't ever try to go to work after a session like that again. Fortunately, he understood and forgave me.

Just like she warned, for the next few days I could not focus and was pretty much worthless. I had to take a few days off work. But slowly, my belief about myself related to the abortion was changing. As a result of the processing, I was able to change my belief to "I am forgiven." Period. End of discussion.

Up until then, I felt like Jesus died for others but that his death on the cross couldn't possibly cover my sin. Not *that* sin. But slowly, my mind began to grasp the truth. Jesus paid the price for all my sin. I may deserve to be punished, but because Jesus hung on the cross in my place, I am spared the punishment. I am forgiven. And because I accept that I am forgiven, I have to think and act like I'm forgiven.

When I tell you that my belief changed, I don't say that lightly. Between God and my counselor and my willingness to believe, my beliefs about myself and the abortion changed at the deepest level. I no longer had to punish myself or be ashamed of what I had done.

After that day of processing the abortion, Satan has never again been able to tell me I am unforgivable. I know that I know that I know I am forgiven. And more importantly, I have forgiven myself. It still hurts to think about what I did, and I will never forget. But I don't feel the need to beat myself up like I did prior to processing this event.

Keep Fighting

Consider it pure joy, my brothers and sisters, whenever you face trials of many kinds, because you know that the testing of your faith produces perseverance.

– James 1:2–3

Do not be anxious about anything, but in every situation, by prayer and petition, with thanksgiving, present your requests to God. And the peace of God, which transcends all understanding, will guard your hearts and your minds in Christ Jesus.

– Philippians 4:6–7

In July of 2019, I felt the need to get baptized. I had been baptized as a child, but I couldn't remember it, so I talked to my pastor about setting a date. The church had a Sunday afternoon service coming up that would take place at a local state park. The pastor said that he was planning to do some baptisms near the end of that service. I signed up and invited my friends and family to be my witnesses.

To me, this act of baptism was a symbol of God washing away the old me. It was a symbol of me embracing my identity in Christ. My mom and my best friend were there along with other friends from school. It was a day I will never forget. I was publicly turning my life over to God, accepting the resurrection story and its implications for my own salvation. I was declaring, once and for all, that I belong to God.

My adoption into his kingdom is unearned and undeserved. But that is how much God loves me. That is how much he loves you too. He wants me despite my skin disease and despite my sins. He wants you despite your imperfections and bad decisions. My adoption into God's family is also irrevocable. Nothing can ever take away who I am to my heavenly Father. God wants you in his family too.

As much as I would love to tell you that my problems are now all solved, that isn't the way this story ends. My life is not perfect. My skin is not healed. I still sin, and I still struggle with negative thoughts. I am afraid sometimes. I worry sometimes. I fight the enemy daily, but the point is . . .

I am in the fight!

I am fighting back!

And I am not doing it alone!

Satan will never stop coming after me, but that's OK. Because I am ready. I have a church family and an even closer small group family. I continue to take medication and go to counseling. I am the child of the one true God, and he loves me with a love that no one can fathom. He has given me tools to help myself, tools that I have hopefully shared with you successfully.

Please do not give up. In fact, get up and get going. Don't try to do too much at once, but make a plan. Take deliberate steps toward getting your relationship with God on the right track. Get involved in a church. Find a Bible study you can join and show up. Seek help through medication and counseling if you need it. There is no shame in needing help.

You are in a battle, but God is bigger than any problem you have, and he alone is the source of healing. That doesn't mean he is going to do it all for you though. You have to seek him, learn about him, and listen to him. You must believe him when he says that you are forgiven and that he loves you. Sometimes it may be a very purposeful choice to believe what God says about you, but it is a choice you have to make. It is the only choice you can make that will lead to victory.

I want to end this book by referring you to the song "God of All My Days" by Casting Crowns. When I first heard this song, it spoke to my heart. It described the give-and-take relationship we need with God. Every time I had a need and took steps toward God, he met me there. What I especially want you to notice is how, with each action we take, God meets us there with an action of his own. I was a poster child for brokenness, shame, fear, and confusion. But when I turned to God, he met me there with grace, mercy, forgiveness, peace, and healing. My favorite part of the song talks about how God relentlessly pursues us and how, no matter what we have done, his grace still covers us.

Doing nothing was easy, but it wasn't helping me get any better. If you and I can muster up the strength to turn to God and take baby steps towards him, he will be there.

God of All My Days
by Casting Crowns

I came to you with my heart in pieces
And found the God with healing in His hands
I turned to You, put everything behind me
And found the God who makes all things new
I looked to You, drowning in my questions
And found the God who holds all wisdom
And I trusted You and stepped out on the ocean
You caught my hand among the waves
'Cause You're the God of all my days

Each step I take
You make a way
And I will give you all my praise
My seasons change, You stay the same
You're the God of all my days

I ran from You, I wandered in the shadows
And found a God who relentlessly pursues
I hid from You, haunted by my failure
And found the God whose grace still covers me
I fell on You when I was at my weakest
And found the God, the lifter of my head
And I've worshiped You
And felt You right beside me
You're the reason that I sing
'Cause You're the God of all my days

In my worry, God You are my stillness
In my searching, God, You are my answers
In my blindness, God, You are my vision
In my bondage, God, You are my freedom
In my weakness, God, You are my power
You're the reason that I sing
'Cause You're the God of all my days

In my blindness, God, You are my vision
In my bondage, God, You are my freedom
All my days

Can You Help?

Thank You for Reading My Book!

I really appreciate all your feedback,
and I love hearing what you have to say.
In exchange for your willingness to leave me
an honest review on Amazon,
I would like to offer you the FREE workbook
I have created to help you with your own journey.
You may access this workbook by visiting
www.toleratednotwanted.com
and providing me your email address.
I will send you a copy of the workbook
in the form of a PDF document.

Again, please leave me an honest review on Amazon
letting me know what you thought of the book.
Thanks so much!
Kathy Smith Carter

Acknowledgments

To my husband Greg: when I came to you and told you that God was asking me to write a book, your immediate response was "Do it!" You sat and listened to me as I read and reread this story with such supportive patience. You encouraged me to be as real as possible and I am so grateful.

◆

To my mom and my sisters: I know some of this was a shock for you and was difficult to read. You never judged me and extended me such grace. Thank you for loving me anyway!

◆

To my friends (Stephanie, Cindy, Jennifer, Laura, Lisa, Devereaux): I heard nothing but excitement in your voices when others showed doubt. Thank you for supporting me through the process of fighting my way back and for encouraging me when life seemed so hopeless.

◆

To my counselor: You played a key role in my healing and I am forever grateful that God sent you to me. You let me cry, pushed me to deal with the past and continually led me to Jesus. You told me truths that I didn't want to hear and challenged me to make healthier choices. Thank you!

◆

And to my heavenly Father: Yours is the only voice that matters. Thank you for sending me these people and for helping lead me out of darkness. The struggle never ceases, but neither does your love. You are bigger than anything I have to face in life. Please use this book to bring someone closer to you.

NOW IT'S YOUR TURN

Discover the EXACT 3-step blueprint you need to become a best-selling author in as little as 3 months.

Self-Publishing School helped me, and now I want them to help you with this FREE resource to begin outlining your book! Even if you're busy, bad at writing, or don't know where to start, you CAN write a bestseller and build your best life. With tools and experience across a variety of niches and professions, Self-Publishing School is the only resource you need to take your book to the finish line!

DON'T WAIT

Say "YES" to becoming a bestseller:

https://self-publishingschool.com/friend/

Follow the steps on the page to get a FREE resource to get started on your book and unlock a discount to get started with Self-Publishing School

About the Author

Kathy Smith Carter is a wife of twenty years, a daughter, a sister, and a mom to three Labradors. She has been an elementary school counselor for 14 years and uses her dogs as therapy dogs in her counseling sessions. She loves college football, Mickey Mouse, and gardening. She was born with a rare skin disease called ichthyosis.

Made in the USA
Las Vegas, NV
19 April 2022